Hip Hop Hooray

Hip Hop Hooray

CELEBRATING 30 YEARS OF RAP MUSIC

Featuring interviews with Hip Hop legends like Kurtis Blow, Dana Dane, Rockmaster Scott and the Dynamic 3, Kokane the Hook Master, Grandmaster Mele Mel, Queen Pen, Arrested Development, and the Fat Boys

By Sean XLG Mitchell

FOREWORD
By Kool Rock Ski *of The Fat Boys*

Colossus Books
An Imprint of Amber Communications Group, Inc.
Phoenix, Arizona

HIP HOP HOORAY
CELEBRATING 30 YEARS OF RAP MUSIC

By Sean XLG Mitchell

Published by:
Colossus Books
An Imprint of Amber Communications Group, Inc.
1334 East Chandler Boulevard, Suite 5-D67
Phoenix, AZ 85048
Amberbk@aol.com
WWW.AMBERBOOKS.COM

Tony Rose, Publisher/Editorial Director
Yvonne Rose, Associate Publisher
Yvonne Shackleford, Associate Editor
The Printed Page, Interior Design / Cover Layout

ALL RIGHTS RESERVED

No part of this book may be used, reproduced or transmitted in any form or by any means—electronic or mechanical, including photocopying, recording or by any information storage and retrieval system without written permission from the author, except for the inclusion of brief quotations in a review or critical article.

COLOSSUS BOOKS are available at special discounts for bulk purchases, sales promotions, fundraising or educational purposes.

Copyright © 2011 by Sean Mitchell and Amber Communications Group, Inc.

ISBN#: 978-1-937269-15-9

Library of Congress Cataloging-in-Publication Data

Mitchell, Sean XLG.
  Hip hop hooray : celebrating 30 years of rap music / Sean XLG Mitchell.
    p. cm.
  "Featuring interviews with Hip Hop legends like Kurtis Blow, Dana Dane, Rockmaster Scott and the Dynamic 3, Kokane the Hook Master, Grandmaster Mele Mel, Queen Pen, Arrested Development, and the Fat Boys."
  Includes bibliographical references and index.
  ISBN 978-1-937269-15-9 (alk. paper)
  1. Rap (Music)--History and criticism. 2. Rap musicians--Interviews. I. Title.
  ML3531.M48 2011
  782.42164909--dc23
                                         2011036335

Dedication

This book is dedicated to the Creator for making all things possible, to the ancestors for their struggles and triumphs, to our leaders for their wisdom and courage, and to the children who are the future-Rock on.

—Sean XLG

Shout Outs

I would like to give a shout out to Zakiya for all your hard work and dedication—one love, my wife Clarissa, Sweet P & K-J "Hipnotik," Tony and Yvonne Rose and Amber Books, Jazzy Jeff and Lady T, Mellow G-Man, Miggie Smalls, Uncle Charles and Aunt Val, Charles, Sherry and Diana Mitchell, Ferrell 'DJ Smooth' Solomon and Vickie, John "Bark" Coston and Sharelle, Big Joe and Ressie Bishop and the Jazzy 5, Sandi, Lea, Shannon, William Jr., Tonya and Kevie Kev Rodgers and Tricia, Ruby Cooper, Tyra and 'Dollar' Bill, Edie and Buddy Bishop, Hubert Jr. Gaddy, Ant Man, Kay-La, Baby "Phat" Dee and Mikey "Jump Shot", my sista Neat, Lorne "LoGo" Goree, Tiff and Wendell, Shirley Lauchie, D-Will, Derrick, Eddie and the 7500 Crew.

Grandmaster Mele Mel, Kurtis Blow, Sweet Tee, Queen Pen, Charlie Prince for showing me love, Rockmaster Scott and the Dynamic Three, Sal Abbatiello, Dana Dane, D. J. Easy Lee of the Treacherous Three, LL Cool J, Chuck D and Foxy 99 FM in Fayetteville, NC, Roots ALC family in DC, Big Mike Alexander, Vicky Leake-Lewis and family, Steve, Andrea, Brittany and Brandon, Percell, Wanda and Justin "Just-Ice," Andres of Black Sheep, Whodini, Kokane, Earnest-you-are-the-man and MNS Media Group, Kaneri Diamond, DJ Suga Rush and the *We Love Radio* show at Pace University, Howard University, David Scheinbaum, Full Force, Christopher 'Play' Martin, Easy A.D., DryerBuzz.com, Chris "the Poetry Man", April Sims and photographer John Mathew Smith.

Finally, to all the Deejays, MCs, graffiti artists, and b-boys all over the world—one love!

Contents

Foreword	x
Introduction	1
One: Yes Yes Y'all…In the Beginning	9
Two: 1982 Flashback	21
Three: Request Line: The Interview with Rockmaster Scott and the Dynamic 3	29
Four: Rock Da House: Interviews	39
Michael Holeman *	39
Sal Abbatiello*	42
Grandmaster Mele Mel*	44
Kurtis Blow	46
Five: 1986 Flashback	51
Six: The Funky Fresh Era	57
Seven: Throw Ya Hands In the Air: Interviews	63
Sweet Tee *	63
Dana Dane *	65
The Fat Boys	69
Hip Hop History in Photos	75
Eight: 1990 Flashback	93
Nine: Bring Da Noise	99

Ten: Pump Up the Bass: Interviews	107
Arrested Development *	107
Kokane the Hook Master	113
Eleven: The Roof Is On Fire	117
Twelve: Rock Da House	131
Thirteen: Getting' Jiggy Wit It: Interviews	141
Kaneri Diamond*	141
Queen Pen*	143
Rosa Clemente	145
Fourteen: Notable Hip Hop Work	151
The Afterword	165
About the Author	169

Foreword

By Kool Rock Ski *of The Fat Boys*

Back in the days when we yearned to be stars
My crew used to jam on them bars
Our microphones came from an old cassette
'Cause we rocked on anything we could get
No lie, we used to emulate the Furious Five
And the Treacherous Three were my favorite MCs
The Cold Crush 4 had rhymes galore
Afrika Bambaataa at the Roxy y'all
If you knew how to flow you got hounded like a shadow
MCs were quick to say, "What's up? You wanna battle"?
Run home and study your rhymes and come back
And man, you got dissed if your shit was wack
I know it well. Brooklyn mad hell
When bro's got killed for a pair of gazelles
When honeys only talked to light-skinned cats
When it was Hip-Hop before they called it Rap

Hip Hop Hooray

Introduction

The style of flashy entertainment first made routine by Motown became the form of Soul music that dominated throughout the 1970s. Disco changed the beat, but not the basic show business emphasis on surface and form rather than content and meaning. At the same time, the values of "artistic expression" in Rock led to the era of superstar indulgence. Punk was the Rock music reaction to this trend and Rap was the Black music parallel to the Punk music. It began emerging at approximately the same time, although it took much longer to be discovered and publicized.

Rap grew out of an impoverished economic environment and the necessity of the ghetto, in all of its unlikely conditions, made it possible. The kids would cart their turntables, amplifiers, mics and records into the park then pry open the electrical boxes at the base of the park lights and tap into the city's power lines. Once the power was turned on, "get on the mic and start to rap" was both the rallying cry and the challenge and the parks and schoolyards of the South Bronx was filled with kids eager to pick it up.

Both Presidents Carter and Reagan traveled to the South Bronx at the start of their terms to have their photos taken while standing in the rubble and promising urban renewal, but in between the presidential visits, the area remained an eyesore of urban ruins. It is a cruel irony that the unreconstructed ghetto status of the South Bronx provided the physical conditions that allowed the developing art of rapping to flourish. Parks and schoolyards there are not the neat and orderly enclosures found in middle-class neighborhoods, which meant they could be used by the rappers and their audience for outdoor competitions with sound systems that gave birth to Rap.

From the parks, rapping moved indoors to parties and dances held at social clubs and the community centers that were built into some Bronx housing projects. This was the circuit that first made the reputations of the early rappers and deejays like Hollywood and Kool DJ Herc. These deejays and rappers developed large followings of kids who would tape their performances on their portable boom boxes. While people like Kool Herc and the Herculoids were deejaying and rapping, people like Grandmaster Flash—the generation of artists who caught the movement's commercial potential—were in the audience.

By 1978, Rap was a major phenomenon in Black New York, having spread from the South Bronx to Manhattan's Harlem and Brooklyn's Bed-Stuy areas. Rap events at clubs like the Dixie and the Black Door attracted hundreds of kids. There was a devoted audience of fans who knew the names and reputations of rappers who were now aligned in three, four, and five man "crews" such as Grandmaster Flash and the Furious 5, Funky 4 + One, Fantastic Five, Crash Crew, and the Treacherous Three. Rap was still a live performance—the only recordings were the cassette tapes made by the fans, however, this was soon to change.

In the Hip-Hop world, 1979 would be the year that brought Rap music into mainstream consciousness. Although "King Tim the III" by the Fat Back Band was the official first Rap song on wax, "Rapper's Delight" by the Sugar Hill Gang spearheaded the way and was an instant classic. The enormous success of the song was unparallel, selling over three million copies and it was certified triple-platinum. The song played in heavy rotation for months on radio stations across the country. The music was the instrumental sounds of the popular R&B hit "Good Times" by Chic. The heavy bass line grooves provided the perfect backbeat to underscore the party theme of the song.

In Black neighborhoods everywhere, you could hear someone singing the phrase "Hip-Hop da hibbit" or "ho-tel, mo-tel, Holiday Inn."

Released by a small independent label called Sugar Hill Records, the label owner and brain behind the early success of Rap music was none other than Sylvia Robinson of "Pillow Talk" fame. Following the path laid by the Sugar Hill Gang, a number of artists hit the scene. The Sequence released "Funk You Up," Grandmaster Flash and the Furious 5 scored underground hits with "We Rap More Mellow" and "Super Rappin'" on the Enjoy record label.

Spoonie Gee came out and made noise with "Spoonin Rap" and Kurtis Blow released the gold single "Christmas Rappin'." Other notable artists that dropped records during the year were the Jazzy 4 M.C.s with "M.C. Rock," Ron Hunt released "Spider Rap," Lady D rocked with a self-titled cut, and Paulette and Tanya Winely did the damn thing with "Rhymin' and Rappin'." This was just the beginning!

Fast forward to the present. In 2008, I had a telephone conversation with Charlie Prince and Slick Rick of Rockmaster Scott and the Dynamic Three. Coincidently, they were scheduled to be the opening act for L.L Cool J the following weekend at a show in Richmond, Virginia. They invited me down to check it out and on the night of the show, I made it down to Brown's Island. I arrived a little late, but was able to hook up with Charlie Prince before he went on stage. Charlie ran through the group's hits "Request Line" and "The Roof Is on Fire" (parts I and II) and had the crowd hyped before he shut it down for L.L.

When L.L. stepped on stage and started his act, I couldn't help but admire his showmanship as I studied his performance. He did hit after hit and never missed a beat. Jams like "Hey Lover," joints off of his latest LP *Exit 13*, and his old classics like "Rock the Bells" and "Boomin' System" turned the show ballistic. L.L. brought his young fans on stage to participate in the act and they loved every minute of it. Simply put, he controlled the crowd. More than anything else, I saw the formula that he used to do it.

What I mean by "formula" is the schematic plan of the show that L.L. developed over the years as a veteran in the game. This was a skill honed from doing shows as an opening act for Run-DMC on the Raising Hell Tour to the Def Jam Tour and all the other performances he's done throughout his career. A skill that was cultivated much like R&B legends Smokey Robinson and Patti Labelle who had been singing for decades. It was now evident in Hip-Hop.

"Hip Hop Hooray: Celebrating 30 Years of Rap Music" highlights and recognizes incredible aspects of Hip-Hop. There are literally thousands of significant moments that are worthy enough to be considered 'great'. Monumental events such as D.J. Jazzy Jeff and the Fresh Prince winning the first Grammy Award to little known facts like the story of how Doug E. Fresh introduced the human beat-box while performing on stage when the sound system went out. Doug E. had to improvise to entertain the crowd by mimicking the sound of the beat with his mouth. Obscure and lesser-known occurrences have similar value within proper context. A perfect example would be a 1981 article in the Village Voice newspaper, which may seem trivial on the surface until you realize that it was the first mainstream newspaper to focus on Hip-Hop.

As a Hip-Hop historian, I searched high and low to recognize the most significant moments and events over the last thirty years. Obviously Sedgewick and Cedar, where Kool D.J. Herc played in the South Bronx, is the birthplace and most eventful moment of the genre. I start from the beginning with Herc, Afrika Bambaataa and Grandmaster Flash and end with modern rappers like Kanye West, T.I., and Lil' Wayne. The greatest moments in Hip-Hop are not listed in any sequential order because that would take away from the essence of a unified perspective and, collectively, the moments are all important and equally deserving of recognition.

In the process of writing this book, I had the privilege and pleasure of speaking with a number of legends and luminaries who share their stories, experiences, and visions throughout these pages. I would like to thank and acknowledge them for their invaluable contributions:

Grandmaster Mele Mel: Three-time Grammy Award-winner and member of the first Rap act, Grandmaster Flash and the Furious Five, to be inducted into the Rock and Roll Hall of Fame.

Sal Abbatiello: Former manager and owner of Hip-Hop's number one club Disco Fever, whose monumental presence is highlighted and recognized in the 1985 hit film *Krush Groove*.

Michael Holman: Hip-Hop entrepreneur and creator of the first Hip-Hop television show *Graffiti Rock*, who, along with Fab Five Freddy, was instrumental in bringing together the four elements of Hip-Hop culture: deejaying, B-boying, graffiti and emceeing.

Rockmaster Scott and Dynamic Three: Pioneer Rap act known for the classic hits "Request Line" and "The Roof Is On Fire" who were also instrumental in launching the careers of Doug E. Fresh and Slick Rick of the Get Fresh Crew.

Kurtis Blow: A Hip Hop legend and the long time King of Rap. He is the first male artist in the history of the music industry to debut with back-to-back gold singles. Kurtis is widely recognized as the first Rap superstar.

Kokane: Kokane, otherwise known as the Hook Master. The L.A./West Coast emcee is widely known as the most featured artist in the history of the music industry with over 1800 guest appearances, including hot joints he's put down with Snoop Dogg like "Go Away" and "Wrong Idea."

Queen Pen: Teddy Riley's protégé and the voice on the Black Street classic hit *No Diggity*, Queen Pen has been one of the most prominent and respected female emcees in the game since her debut in the 90s.

Sweet Tee: One of the first successful solo female emcees in the game whose hits include "It's My Beat" and "On the Smooth Tip." She is highly regarded as one of the tightest female lyricists ever.

Dana Dane: The first Brooklyn-bred solo emcee to go gold with his 1987 smash LP "Dana Dane with Fame." Known for his clever storytelling and witty lyrics, Dana Dane, along with former Rap partner MC Ricky D, popularized the art of storytelling and scored big hits with "Nightmares" and "Cinderfella Dana Dane."

The Fat Boys: One of the most successful Hip-Hop acts of all time, the Fat Boys scored major hits including the single "Fat Boys," "Jail House Rap," "Sex Machine," and the crossover sensation "Wipe Out," to name a few. They are the first Rap act to star in their own major motion film, *Disorderlies*.

Arrested Development: This Grammy Award-winning Rap act is one of the first to put the South on the map. Representing ATL, their alternative Hip-Hop style proved successful with the mega hits "Tennessee" and "People Everyday."

Additional contributing artists include: Sparky D, Hitman Howie Tee, Joeski Love, Grand Wizard Theodore, Reggie Reg from the Crash Crew, Fearless 4, Jimmy Spicer, Mercedes Ladies, Educated Rapper from UTFO, Positive K, Donald D from Rhyme Syndicate, Pow Wow from Soul Sonic Force, and Cut Master Cool V who is the cousin of and deejay for Biz Markie.

> *Yeah, at one point I had met Flash up at the 371 Club. I was looking for a deejay at that time. Flash was looking for an emcee and he was like, "I need an emcee. Can you come and emcee for me?" So I got down with Flash and we were rocking for a while. Then Mele Mel came around and it was Kurtis Blow and Mele Mel! Wow! Mele Mel and I was partners for maybe a year and then all the Furious came back and they put me down. I was actually the seventh member. The sixth emcee was a guy I went to the School of Music and Arts with. His name was Kool Kyle (The Star Child). Grandmaster Flash and the Furious 7, we were like the Earth, Wind, and Fire of Hip-Hop.*
>
> —Kurtis Blow

Introduction

Pac is not here. People don't know I was with him two days before he got killed, me and Suge. I was on the set with him and Jim Belushi (Gang Related) and we were starting this thing together called One Nation with Spice 1.

—Kokane

Hip Hop Hooray

One

Yes Yes Y'all...The Beginning

Maximum Occupancy: 3,000

On September 2, 1978 at the Audubon Ballroom in New York City, New York there was a sign on the door from the New York City Fire Department that read: "Maximum Occupancy: 3,000." There had never been a Rap show in front of a crowd this large. It was 1978, Rap had yet to make it to records, and the only performances were at the parks and clubs like The Black Door and The Dixie. However, this was the night that changed Hip-Hop forever. Grandmaster Flash and The Furious Four built such a huge following in the Bronx and Uptown with a reputation as the kings of this new art form called Hip-Hop that they headlined the show and performed before a sold-out audience, rocking the house with Flash on the wheels of steel and the four emcees kickin' rhymes and routines with a style that exploded on stage and set a new course for Hip-Hop venues!

International Flavor

In Brazil, 1981, an outdoor concert was scheduled to jump off. This was not a typical event in Brazil where you might expect to hear the soulful sounds of Forro, a Jazz-Funk combination of dance music infused with traditional rhythms of the natives. This, however, was the country's first Hip-Hop show featuring the Harlem-based trio better known as The Treacherous Three. The outdoor event drew an astonishing crowd of over 60,000 people. D.J. Easy Lee along with the three emcees—Kool Moe Dee, Special K, and L.A. Sunshine turned the show out with their devastating performance. This event not only took place on foreign territory in terms of Hip-Hop venues, but it happened within the second year of recorded Rap music and, to this day, is one of the largest outdoor concerts for a single Rap act.

> *My greatest moment in Hip-Hop history was when Soul Sonic Force got in the studio and did Planet Rock!*
> —Pow Wow, Afrika Bambaataa, and the Soul Sonic Force

Magnifico

Latinos have always been a major part in the development of Hip-Hop from break-dancing to graffiti, deejaying, and emceeing. D.J. Charlie Chase of the Cold Crush Brothers was one of the first Latino deejays and he built a solid reputation throughout the South Bronx during the early years of Hip-Hop. Grand Wizard Theodore and the Fantastic Five, known for their 1981 cut, "Can I Get A Soul Clap" and most notably their appearance in the 1983 movie *Wild Style*, introduced two of the first Latinos in the world of rap—Prince Whipper Whip and Ruby D. However, the mainstream breakthrough, in terms of recognition, occurred in the summer of 1981 with the song, "Disco Dream" by the Rap crew Mean Machine. Set to the funky bass line of "Pull Up To The Bumper" by Grace Jones, "Disco Dream" featured verses of Spanish Rap by group member Mr. Schick and the song became a huge hit and instant classic. This song opened the doors to a large Puerto Rican fan base, which led to the eventual success of such stars as Tito from Fearless 4, Prince Markie Dee from the Fat Boys, Big Pun, Fat Joe, Cypress Hill, Cam'ron, and dozens of graf artists, emcees, deejays, and b-boys!

The Place To Be

For Classical music, it's Carnegie Hall; for Opera, it's the Met; for Country music, it's the Grand Old Opry; and that's exactly what the Disco Fever was to Hip-Hop. This is the one club that held every major Rap act at one time and was the dream of up-and-coming rappers to perform there. Although a number of other clubs were hot on the circuit like The 371 Club, the Dixie, and the Black Door in the early years, in terms of heavyweight performances, The Disco Fever was in a class by itself. The popularity of the Disco Fever was so significant that in 1985, the club was used to film performances in the major motion picture *Krush Groove*. Sal Abbatiello, former manger and owner of the club, is a legend in the world of Hip-Hop and was instrumental in the early success of artists such as Kurtis Blow, Sweet G, Grandmaster Flash, Run-DMC, the Fat Boys and Hip-Hop entrepreneur Russell Simmons.

That's the Breaks

The release of Kurtis Blow's singles, "Christmas Rappin'" and "The Breaks" made music history. In 1979, Blow exploded on the music scene and by 1980, with the success of his two songs, he became the first male artist in history to debut with back-to-back gold singles. The two songs were also the first Rap records to be released on a major label, Mercury. The success of these songs were followed by a string of hits that included, "Party Time," "It's Tough," "Basketball," and "If I Ruled The World." Kurtis became the first star in the Rap game with hit songs, interviews, and appearances on mainstream television shows like ABC's 20/20, The Phil Donahue Show, and Soul Train, and was the first rapper to appear in a commercial which was a soft drink ad for Sprite in 1986.

Let's Talk About Sex

The origin of Love Rap had its beginnings with Spoonie Gee. As an MC, Spoonie built his career on rhymes that were directed to girls. "Love Rap," as well as his other popular songs, described his adventures of meeting and picking up girls and describing himself as the king of romance. However, Spoonie did this with a braggadocio style while using the same type of music tracks as a party record. It was primarily about sex, but it was the first scenario of bringing male/female relationships into the equation of a Rap song.

As far as a romantic style of love Rap, Whodini was the first to do it. The first release from their self-titled debut album in 1983 was a song called "Yours For A Night." The music had a strong R&B feel to it, a singing chorus, and the lyrics, "I want to be yours, I belong to you, my heart my soul and my body too." Of course, years later, Whodini scored a huge hit with "One Love" and the following year, L.L. Cool J defined his career with "I Need Love," influencing several other rappers to venture down this path.

The Legendary Battle

New Years, 1980. Kool Moe Dee versus Busy Bee. The battle resulted from a challenge at Harlem World's annual Rap contest that Kool Moe Dee hosted while Busy Bee was a contestant. Busy Bee was known as a house rocker and a crowd favorite who was undefeated in MC contests up until this point. However, the showdown between the two emcees ended with Kool Moe Dee crushing Busy Bee in front of a jam-packed house at Harlem World. "…Yo, Busy Bee, I don't mean to be bold/but put the bob diddy bob bull shit on hold…" and the crowd just lost its mind!

Village Voice

During the week of April 22 in 1981, the Village Voice, a weekly newspaper in New York, featured an article on break-dancing. Written by Sally Banes, the story was titled, "Physical Graffiti; Breaking Is Hard To Do." The significance of the story is the time and era in which it took place. In 1981, Rap music was widely considered a fad and most Rap artists were shunned by Black radio with the exception of the Sugarhill Gang and Kurtis Blow. Record labels were not offering Rap artists album deals and they were not promoting tours. Ultimately, the ground-swelling movement of Hip-Hop could not be denied and the article was an early sign of Hip-Hop's mainstream appeal.

My greatest moment in Hip-Hop was in 1988. We were invited to the Grammys, coming on the heels of the success from the Crushin' album, and we sat in the front row and Michael Jackson performed, "Man in the Mirror" and at the end of the show, somebody came and invited us on the stage for the grand finale with the other acts that performed that night. Michael Jackson just turned to us and shook our hands and he said how much he admired us. He told us how hard we worked and he said, "When I turn on my TV, you guys are everywhere!" We were on cloud 9 then. We were driving home saying, "Michael Jackson just gave us props!

— Kool Rock, the Fat Boys

The Freestyle Flow

At first my pen brings
A burst like ginseng
Of high powered rhymes
Grab the mic and then bring
New styles for miles
With thoughts deep as fossils
A diesel with a premium
Flow like a nozzle
They can only clone sheep
Cause my microphone keeps
A style too hard to copy
So bad it's bone deep
So dictionaries had to be
Rewritten and corrected
The word *phenomenon*
Since this was perfected
A flow so dangerous
Some might even ask
When I'm kicking skills
Do I wear a ski mask
Load mics with rhymes
Take aim and empty 'em
The new world order
For the next millennium
The microphone was checked
And wrecked by a barrage
Of rhymes that had it towed
To the nearest garage
In 2000 years
They'll marvel at remains
When they unearth mics
And find my style under stains

Our song 'Request Line,' if people listen to it, it's more like a Rap-R&B. We were one of the first artists to put Rap and R&B together.

—Charlie Prince of Rockmaster Scott
and the Dynamic Three

The Hip-Hop Battle Royal

July 4, 1981 marks the date of the memorable event that took place at Harlem World between the Cold Crush Brothers and the Fantastic Five. For a $1,000.00 grand prize, winner takes all, the Cold Crush Brothers, donned in pinstriped gangster suits, went head-to-head in a battle with the tuxedo-clad Fantastic Five. The showdown in front of a jam-packed crowd exemplified rhyme techniques and showmanship at its best. When it was all said and done, the Fantastic Five were voted as the winners. To date, this battle remains as one of the most classic moments in Hip-Hop. Fast-forward to 1987 when Kool Moe Dee engaged in a legendary battle with L.L. Cool J with a series of dis records that started with Kool Moe Dee's "How Ya Like Me Now" and zenithed with L.L.'s song "Moma Said Knock You Out." The outcome of the battle remains in controversy as to who won, but Hip-Hop promoter Van Silk offered them a challenge to battle for one million dollars on a nationally televised Pay-Per-View event. Kool Moe Dee accepted the challenge, but L.L. declined the offer, so we may never know who would've walked away the victor.

That's The Joint

In February of 1981, the Funky Four Plus One made Hip-Hop history. The group, known for their hits, "Rappin' and Rockin' the House," "That's The Joint," "Do You Wanna Rock," and "Feel It (The Mexican)" became the first Rap act to perform on national television. As musical guests on the hit television show *Saturday Night Live*, the Funky Four Plus One hit the stage in front of the world and did the damn thing!

The Magic Rap Attack

April 15, 1979 is the date when *Mr. Magic's Rap Attack* hit the air for the first time. The show, hosted by Brooklyn-bred DJ Mr. Magic on WHBI's radio station, broadcasted from out of Newark, New Jersey. In 1982, WBLS Program Director Frankie Crocker brought Mr. Magic on board to host a weekend Hip-Hop show and within a year, WBLS became the most listened-to station in the country. Whodini immortalized Mr. Magic in the 1982 hit song "Magic's Wand."

Zulu Nation

Pioneering DJ Afrika Bambaataa founded the Zulu Nation in the mid 1970s. The Nation comprised of hundreds of Black and Latino youth, many of whom were from street gangs throughout the Bronx like the Black Spades. Following Bam's transition into music, the Zulu Nation converted a number of its members into the Hip-Hop movement and they became DJs, MCs, B-boys, and Graffiti artists. Today, the Zulu Nation remains a powerful organization that stands for unity, peace, justice, and equality for all and has chapters in many cities throughout the United States and abroad. Afrika Bambaataa, along with the Jazzy 5 and the Soul Sonic Force, released the classic hits "Jazzy Sensation," "Planet Rock," and "Looking For The Perfect Beat." In 1984, they performed their hit "Frantic Situation" in the major motion film *Beat Street*.

My greatest moment in Hip-Hop history is when Run-DMC & Jam Master Jay were being inducted in the Rock-n-Roll Hall of Fame.

—Joe Ski Love

Two of the greatest shows I ever did have to be a part of a NWA concert. I've seen a whole lot of concerts, been on tour and everything, and there was nobody that made an impact like NWA. When they came out and said 'Fuck the Police,' you talk about hype!

—Kokane

The Sweet Taste of Success

The group The Disco Three won their first recording contract in a Rap contest with Tin Pan Apple in 1983. Shortly afterwards, they released their first single called "Reality," a song with a serious underlying message. Their next release, a song entitled "Fat Boys," shot up the charts and the group became a household name. The success of the song led the group to change their name to The Fat Boys and the rest was music history. The group, consisting of members Prince Markie Dee, Kool Rockski, and Buffy the Human Beat Box, had a combined weight of nearly 1,000 pounds. They went on to release several platinum and gold albums and a string of hits to include the crossover sensation "Wipe Out," a remake with the original artists, The Beach Boys. In making mockery of their enormous sizes, The Fat Boys became the first Rap act with a successful gimmick. In 2010, the Fat Boys were featured on TV One's show *Unsung*.

Wild Style

In 1983, Charlie Ahearn had a vision to put Hip-Hop on the silver screen and partnered up with graffiti legend Fab Five Freddy to bring the vision into reality. Their collaboration lead to the masterpiece we all know as *Wild Style*, Hip-Hop's first and finest movie flick. The film showcased the elements of the culture in its authentic form: the DJ, the

Break-Dancer, the M.C., and the Graffiti Artist. The movie features legendary acts from the Cold Crush Brothers, Fantastic Freaks, and Busy Bee to Electric Force, Rock Steady, and Grandmaster Flash. The climax was a live performance at the Amphitheatre featuring Double Trouble, Cold Crush, Busy Bee, and Fantastic Freaks, a show that many would call the Woodstock of Hip-Hop.

> *My greatest moment was when Hip-Hop became recognized as a music genre at the Grammy Awards after it was boycotted. Fresh Prince and Jazzy Jeff were the first to be honored.*
> —Reggie Reg from Crash Crew

Hall of Fame Hits

"SELF DESTRUCTION"—KRS-ONE & VARIOUS ARTISTS

"HEY D.J."—WORLD'S FAMOUS SUPREME TEAM

"CHILDREN'S STORY"—SLICK RICK

"HEY YA!"—OUTKAST

"BASKETBALL"—KURTIS BLOW

"GIN AND JUICE"—SNOOP DOGGY DOG

"LEX, COOPS, BIMAZ AND BENZ"—THE LOST BOYZ

"C.R.E.A.M."—WU TANG CLAN

"A GOOD DAY"—ICE CUBE

"ROCKIN IT"—FEARLESS FOUR

"NO DIGGITY"—BLACK STREET FEATURING DR. DRE & QUEEN PEN

"SOUL SURVIVOR"—YOUNG JEEZY

"I GET THE JOB DONE"—BIG DADDY KANE

"PARTY UP"—DMX

Hip Hop Hooray

Two

1982 Flashback

Amid all the success and popularity of Rap, this became a perilous time for the art form. For the previous 30 years or so, Black music was primarily an R&B market and Rap was beginning to impede on this age-old tradition. Sounds of artists like the Commodores and Donna Summers—acts that had been around for years—were slowly giving way to the sounds of a craft that was honed on the streets of the ghetto. The word "backlash" would be an understatement considering the amount of criticism that grew towards Rap music. All of a sudden, Rap was a "fad" that wouldn't last any longer than two years. People were saying, "It all sounds alike" and that Rap wasn't "real talent."

Much of the criticism aimed towards Rap was done out of spite and out of a lack of understanding from an older crowd that really couldn't relate to the music. However, the one comment "It all sounds alike" actually had a ring of truth. Most Rap records had a party theme with crowd participation and there was not much variation from one song to the next. Acts like Count Coolout, a comical storyteller, and Blowfly, an x-rated rapper, deviated from the norm, but they were more or less novelty acts. For the most part, Rap was at a standstill in terms of creativity.

The top stories in the news in 1982 centered around the following headlines: The tragic death of Princess Grace; John Hinckley, Jr. being found not guilty by reason of insanity in the shooting of President Reagan; San Francisco's 49'ers won the Super Bowl; The Los Angeles

Lakers were the NBA champions; Actor John Belushi of the famed Blues Brothers died of a drug overdose; E.T. was the box office movie of the year; and Michael Jackson's *Thriller* sells more than 25 million copies, becoming the biggest selling album in history. Aside from the mega-hits released from the *Thriller* album, Black radio rocked with the tunes of Aretha Franklin's "Jump To It," "Momma Used To Say" by Junior, "Sexual Healing" by Marvin Gaye, and "A Night To Remember" by Shalamar.

This is the year that I would say Hip-Hop had its second paradigm shift. The first shift was the transformation of rocking parties with a live performance to making records. Making records required an entirely different mindset because a live show was visual and a record was strictly audio. A live show consisted of routines in terms of rhymes, stage presence, and showmanship, whereas records dealt with production, subject matter, verses, and sing-a-long hooks, which was further compounded by creating an image like dress attire, look, etc. and the record company's ability to promote and distribute the song. Nevertheless, '82 was one of the most significant years in Hip-Hop.

There were three major records that came out this year that not only revived, but also pushed Rap into the forefront of Black music. "Planet Rock" by Afrika Bambaataa and the Soul Sonic Force was one of the three records. "Planet Rock" introduced a new techno-funk sound that rocked the summer of '82. The computer style of music with chant-like rhymes gave this song a different feel and flavor on the radio and in the clubs while crossing over to the Pop charts. The futuristic dance track of "Planet Rock," a certified gold single, not only influenced a number of similar songs that followed like "Electric Kingdom," "Get Tough," and "Scorpio," but was the starting point for what is known as the Miami Bass Sound.

The next of the three records was "The Message" by Grandmaster Flash and the Furious 5. This seven-minute commentary on the struggles of ghetto life forever changed the lyrical format of Rap music. The doors were now open for political and social issues to be addressed in a Rap song. "Don't push me cause I'm close to the edge" is one of the most popular and powerful phrases in Hip-Hop history. The song featured the vocal and lyrical talents of Melle Mel and special guest Duke Bootee. "The Message" sold over half a million copies in 18 days and was eventually certified as double-platinum. This song broke down social barriers for Rap music and single-handily established respect for Rap as a legitimate art form. What's more, "The Message" raised the bar for lyrical proficiency for every rapper in the game.

> *Broken glass everywhere*
> *People pissing on the stairs*
> *You know they just don't care*
> *I can't take the smell*
> *Can't take the noise*
> *Got no money to move out*
> *I guess I got no choice.*

Rolling Stone Magazine called "The Message" "The most detailed and devastating report from underclass America since Bob Dylan decried the lonesome death of Hattie Carol." Robert Hilburn of *the Los Angeles Times* called the song "The most noteworthy single of 1982...A revolutionary seven-minute record, 'The Message' is a brilliantly compact chronicle of the tension and despair of the ghetto life that rips at the innocence of the American dream." Ken Tucker of *The Philadelphia I*nquirer called Grandmaster Flash "As important an artist as Pop music has right now." "The Message" became the first Rap record to be played on White Rock radio stations and the first to top Billboard's Black music chart. In England, it made it into the top five of the national charts. It was the first sign of Rap's crossover potential.

The last of the three records is the lesser known, but equally powerful "NBA Rap" by Hurt 'em Bad and the SC Band. Most people have never heard of this song unless they were in Hip-Hop circles at the time it came out. This song was quickly pulled off of shelves due to legalities concerning the music of One Way's hit "Cutie Pie."

Nevertheless, "NBA Rap" was one of the hottest selling records during the first few weeks of its release. It was also one of the most requested songs on radio stations across the country. To show the impact of the song, I went to a record store to buy it three weeks in a row and it was sold out every time before being pulled off the shelves. The store clerk told me it was the hottest selling record in the store and this was in North Carolina!

What makes this song significant is the fact that it introduced a sports theme to the world of Rap and further broadened the creative landscape. The general consensus was that if you could rap about basketball, then you could literally rap about anything. There was no topic that was untouchable. Hurt'em Bad went on to record other songs about sports like "Monday Night Football" and "The Boxing Game" with fairly marginal success and even though the concept was no longer new, Kurtis Blow scored a huge hit two years later with his song "Basketball." This is a testament to how powerful of an idea "NBA Rap" was in 1982.

Other notable events in 1982 include when Whodini hit the scene and enjoyed success with their hit "Magic's Wand," a song dedicated to radio jock Mr. Magic, and was the first Rap song to feature a music video. The legendary Cold Crush Brothers debuted with their single "The Weekend." Grand Mixer DST with the Infinity Rappers released "Grand Mixer Cuts It Up" and Busy Bee rocked with "Making Cash Money." The two biggest hits that rocked the streets and left them smoking were "Rockin' It" by the Fearless 4 and "Breaking Bells" by the Crash Crew with the harmonizing hook:

> We came here tonight to throw down
> So spread the word all around town
> The rap will have you stomping your feet
> To the sounds of the funky breaking bells beat

Afrika Bambaataa and the Soul Sonic Force returned with the mega hit "Looking For The Perfect Beat." Likewise, Grandmaster Flash and the Furious 5 came back with the hits "Scorpio" and "Flash To The Beat." As if that wasn't enough, Melle Mel and Duke Bootee scored on their own with "Message II (Survival)," making Grandmaster Flash and the Furious 5 the top Rap act in Hip-Hop. Whodini, the first Rap group to perform with live dancers, followed the success of "Magic's Wand" with the top twenty hit "Haunted House of Rock," a comical song with a monster theme that could rival Michael Jackson's Thriller.

West Street Mob hit the scene with the dance tune "Ooh Baby," Sequence rocked with "Simon Says," and Kurtis Blow made noise with the release of "Tough." The Sugarhill Gang enjoyed moderate success with "The Lover In You," a smooth tune with a combination of singing and rapping. The Treacherous Three scored hits with "Whip It," a cover of the Dazz Band's hit "Let It Whip" and "Yes We Can-Can," a rap with a message. The Disco 4 made noise as well with "Whip Rap," their version of the Dazz Band's hit. The Fearless Four scored with "It's Magic" and Jimmy Spicer rocked with the popular jam "The Bubble Bunch."

Funky 4 Plus 1 dropped the street favorite "Do You Want To Rock (Before I Let Go)." Pieces of A Dream, known as one of the top jazz bands in the business, ventured into Hip-Hop and scored a popular hit with Mt. Airy Groove and Just 4 came out with "Jam To Remember." The Disco Four dropped the popular cut "Country Rock & Rap" and also made noise with the single "We're At The Party." The Jonzun Crew rode the charts with their hit "Space Cowboy" and the jam all over the streets was the hot dance record "Funky Soul Makossa" by Nairobi featuring the Awesome Foursome. This was one of the hottest underground hits of the year.

More than anything else, 1982 was most noted for the major motion picture *Wild Style*. Wild Style was a feature length movie on Hip-Hop highlighting the various aspects of the culture from deejaying and graffiti to break dancing and rapping. Grandmaster Flash made a cameo appearance rocking on the wheels of steel and rappers like Double Trouble, Cold Crush Brothers, Busy Bee, and Fantastic 5 displayed the art of emceeing with live freestyles and battles. The movie was authentic in as much as showcasing Hip-Hop in its purest form. Although the movie wasn't a blockbuster hit by Hollywood's standards, it was the Godfather in the world of Hip-Hop.

The Sweet Taste of Success

The group The Disco Three won their first recording contract in a Rap contest with Tin Pan Apple in 1983. Shortly afterwards, they released their first single called "Reality," a song with a serious underlying message. Their next release, a song entitled "Fat Boys," shot up the charts and the group became a household name. The success of the song led the group to change their name to The Fat Boys and the rest was music history. The group, consisting of members Prince Markie Dee, Kool Rockski, and Buffy the Human Beat Box, had a combined weight of nearly 1,000 pounds. They went on to release several platinum and gold albums and a string of hits to include the crossover sensation "Wipe Out," a remake with the original artists, The Beach Boys. In making mockery of their enormous sizes, The Fat Boys became the first Rap act with a successful gimmick. In 2010, the Fat Boys were featured on TV One's show *Unsung*.

Wild Style

In 1983, Charlie Ahearn had a vision to put Hip-Hop on the silver screen and partnered up with graffiti legend Fab Five Freddy to bring the vision into reality. Their collaboration lead to the masterpiece we all know as *Wild Style*, Hip-Hop's first and finest movie flick. The film showcased the elements of the culture in its authentic form: the DJ, the Break-Dancer, the M.C., and the Graffiti Artist. The movie features legendary acts from the Cold Crush Brothers, Fantastic Freaks, and Busy Bee to Electric Force, Rock Steady, and Grandmaster Flash. The climax was a live performance at the Amphitheatre featuring Double Trouble, Cold Crush, Busy Bee, and Fantastic Freaks, a show that many would call the Woodstock of Hip-Hop.

1982 Flashback

My greatest moment was when Hip-Hop became recognized as a music genre at the Grammy Awards after it was boycotted. Fresh Prince and Jazzy Jeff were the first to be honored.
—Reggie Reg from Crash Crew

Hip Hop Hooray

Three

The Interview with Rockmaster Scott and the Dynamic 3

Request Line

DJ, please pick up your phone. I'm on the request line.
Hey Charlie Prince on your request line
I would like to know your name and your zodiac sign
Say what? You're a Scorpio just like me
And I'd like to let you know that I'm nasty
If you give me a chance with you, fly girl,
I'd bet you any amount of money I can rock your world
'Cause when I'm in the mood to get things done
The whole town is the place. We can have big fun
And if it doesn't sound right and you don't agree,
Let's go to my house 'cause I got the key
I don't have a water bed and the reason why
Because it's not necessary. No need to lie
So if you wanna be my girl, you must come correct
And you might be the girl that I would select
In the heavens above known to be the prince of love
When it comes to meeting me, you don't have to shove
DJ, please pick up your phone. I'm on the Request Line

The Interview

Q. Who were the artists that influenced you guys when you were coming up in Hip-Hop?

A. Cold Crush and Fantastic Five.

Q. What about Grandmaster Flash and the Furious Five?

A. Flash and the Furious 5 were like the main pioneers of it all. How can I put it? When it came down to that Rap thing, they were pretty much like the first. Melle Mel at that particular time was the top dog. Nobody could beat Mel.

Q. What year did you guys get started?

A. As far as recording, we got started in '83, but as far as rapping, we started out around '78, '79.

Q. In 1984, you guys rocked the world with your classic hits "Request Line" and "The Roof Is On Fire." "The Roof Is On Fire" has been used a thousand times on TV and in movies like *House Party* with Kid 'N Play and everywhere else you can imagine. Now, is your group being acknowledged as the originators of the phrase "The Roof Is On Fire?"

A. I would say no and yeah. I say no because, a lot of times, when people use the song, I would think they would want us to feature due to the fact that they used the song on one of their tracks or one of their videos. But on the other hand, they do give us credit because they have to pay us to use it. I think we do get the recognition because of the fact that everybody sat there and used the song all over the world no matter what it was; whether it was Heavy Metal, Rock, or Rap—whatever the case may be. They threw it in their movies, they threw it in their TV shows, they threw it in their cup of coffee and ice tea. They used that song and we are considered blessed for that. To think of our song out of all songs to sit there and use, that's a true blessing.

Q. In May of 2007, your group was pictured in *Jet* magazine for receiving an ASCAP Award. Do you think more should be done to acknowledge the old school's contribution to Hip-Hop?

A. We got that ASCAP award and that was for the Latinos. They gave us an ASCAP Award for best songwriters of the year.

Q. In the last few years, VH1 has paid tribute to Rap artists at the Hip-Hop Honors. Artists like Ice-T, Run-DMC, Grandmaster Flash and the Furious 5, Tupac, and Snoop. Have they scheduled you guys to appear on the Hip-Hop Honors show?

A. Not at all. During that time, Missy Elliott was on one of those shows and she was being honored and she came out with "Work It," which had "Request Line" at the beginning of the song. When she came out, that should've been us right there with her due to the fact that she used our sample.

Q. Now, your group not only put the label Reality Records on the map with your hit song "It's Life (You Gotta Think Twice)" in 1983, but you're also responsible for helping to launch the careers of Doug E Fresh, M.C. Ricky D (Slick Rick), and the Get Fresh Crew. Can you elaborate on how all of that went down and the confusion regarding the name Slick Rick?

A. (Slick Rick) Well, during the course of the time, Charlie and I and the rest of the group were doing shows before we became artists—we did quite a few shows. They had a lot of battles back in those days and they used to have a lot of battles in Harlem World. We used to go to Harlem World and each time we went to battle, so we were in competition and that's where we met Dougie at—he was a solo artist. He was in those battles as well. He was cool. He used to make us laugh on stage. He was like a comedy rapper. He used to say stuff like, "Bang ya head against the wall." The crowd was ready for him to say, "Throw ya hands in the air" and he was setting them up by saying, "Bang ya head against the wall." He used to make us laugh with that.

Now, how I met Rick is he came into the Bronx one day along with Dana Dane, who was with a group called the Kangol Crew, I think. They came around in my neighborhood and at that time, I was with my first love and how I met him is they managed to see each other and they embraced each other and everything and I was like, "Who is this?" So he introduced himself as Ricky D and I said, "Oh really? Well, I'm Ricky D, so how are there two emcees named Ricky D in the Rap game?" But I said, "It's cool. We got the same name. We ain't got no big career out of it." He's in Manhattan somewhere rocking at that particular time or Brooklyn and I'm all the way in the Bronx bouncing back and forth to Manhattan and I guess we never bumped heads.

At that time when we were doing shows in the city, we were traveling with the Cold Crush Brothers and Fantastic 5. Back in those days, that was considered big, so we was pretty much big time, so I was looking at Rick like, "Yeah, you ain't gonna make it kid" and I never would've thought he would come right behind me. Now, I'm not sure how he and Dougie connected, but somewhere down the line after we made our first song, "It's Life (You Gotta Think Twice)" with Reality Records and then Profile picked that up. I never sat down and heard of those guys anymore.

All of sudden, here it is 1984 and we're getting ready to record our song with Reality Records and it dropped, "The Roof is On Fire" b/w "Request Line," our first single. Okay, we did our thing and made our money. Our producer, who is also the label owner, came to us and said, "What do you think about this song?" So he plays the song and we were like, "Damn! This is hot. That's Dougie?!" They said, "Yeah, that's Doug." We all listen to it and say, "That's hot. Yeah, we know Doug from Harlem World. That's the 'bang your head against the wall' kid. Yeah, we know Doug. That's hot. Oh yeah, he got that kid, Ricky D, on there."

I had changed my name to Slick Rick, so I was like, okay, he's Ricky D and I'm Slick Rick. We're cool now. "So what do you think about the song?" "We like the song." "You all think it's good enough for me to sign them?" "Yeah, sign those kids. We know them. We're all right with them. We go way back to Harlem World. Put them down." So he signed them with no hesitation due to the fact that we sat there and approved it and the song was hot. Here comes Doug and Rick, they're out doing their thing and that's how it happened.

Q. Is Hip-Hop dead?

A. It is what it is. I'm starting to agree with him [Nas] now. When I listen to the Rap today my kids listen to, I'm confused. The way I see it is there's two ways to die, mentally and physically and once you're dead mentally, it ain't long before physical death claims you. When you listen to Rap, the way it was back then, it's nothing like the way it is now. And the way Rap is today, it's basically killing the mentality of the children today. When he said Hip-Hop is dead, it is killing the children because it's putting negative thoughts in their head leading to violence. Back in the day, it was all about a party, "throw ya hands in the air," you know, having a good time and we were saying "fly girls and fly guys" and today, they're saying "bitches and niggas." And then it got to the point where guys are running around saggin' in the back and when you look at the word saggin' in reverse, you got the word niggas.

Q. What would you guys say is your greatest moment in Hip-Hop?

A. (Charlie Prince) My greatest moment in Hip-Hop is when "Request Line" started taking off to another level. The funny thing about that is our song was so hot they wanted us in two places at the same time. Me and Scott went to Fayetteville (North Carolina) and Rick and MBG went to Brooklyn. They had the tough crowd.

Hip Hop Hooray

Q. How would you like for history to remember Rock Master Scott and the Dynamic Three?

A. One of the greatest, timeless groups that was ever created. I want them to remember us in the Hall of Fame with a new saying, "The roof is on fire!" It's a slogan now—something that should be in the Hip-Hop Hall of Fame. They got a wax museum they're getting ready to build in the Bronx and we're one of the groups that are going to be waxed.

My greatest moment in Hip-Hop is when Big Daddy Kane did a show at Madison Square Garden and asked me to open up for him. The arena was sold out and the place was packed. I did my hit 'What Your Man Gotta Do With Me?' and the crowd was so loud I couldn't understand what they were screaming and after I finished my performance, I passed the mic. to Biggie and he did his freestyle.

—Positive K

My greatest moment in Hip-Hop, I would have to say, is when I performed at the Grammys with Chaka Khan for the song "I Feel For You." The song won a Grammy Award for record of the year and an American Music Award and went platinum.

—Grandmaster Mele Mel

The Interview with Rockmaster Scott and the Dynamic 3

"One thing I love about Hip-Hop is that it's more than just an industry; It is really a culture. Until you really live it like I have lived it, you wouldn't understand it. It's been a part of my life, not just the music that I listen to, not just the way I dance, not just the graffiti art I love to look at; it's a way of life. It's in your heart."

—Kurtis Blow

Armageddon

Too much for a mic
My rhymes need a rocket launcher
For lines that'll redefine
The musical genre
With hollow point skills
That'll rip mesh to flesh
And leave an acrid smell of smoke
'Til the air's no longer fresh
'Cause for years I studied the pen
Like it was Zen
Learned all there is to know
About a flow and then
Mastered many techniques
and put 'em to use
Now you feel like your mind
Is in the hands of a masseuse
When it comes to a battle
It's whatever shows bring
I'll rip the hole from your hinny
And leave you with a nose ring
Your career in a casket
It's just that drastic
Any time you wanna step
Dial 1-800 Ass-kick
Sprayed with shrapnel

Hip Hop Hooray

And getting' hit with rhymes
If the stage was Kosovo
It would be war crimes
'Cause you already f'ed up
And nothing' can save ya'
But right now your mouth
Can do your backside a favor
If you shut up that dumb sh*t
Your ass would be thankful
'Cause I'll pull out the knee cap
And only leave the ankle
So take that stank breath
Gargle and swoosh
Lick smack a Tic-Tac
Then your mouth needs to douche
Now your mic gotta
Handicap sticker stuck on it
'Cause when you grab it, rabbit,
You ain't sayin fu*k on it
You couldn't cover your flaws
With a paint brush
Never heard a mother fu*ker
On the mic I can't crush
My style is Mauy Tai
I'm a war zone survivor
Spittin' flows as if
I had poison in my saliva

Hall of Fame Hits

"WOO HAH (GOT YOU ALL IN CHECK)"—BUSTA RHYMES

"MR. BIG STUFF"—HEAVY D AND THE BOYZ

"GET LOW"—LIL JON AND THE EASTSIDE BOYS

"I GO TO WORK"—KOOL MOE DEE

"JOY AND PAIN"—ROB BASE & DJ EZ ROCK

"BIG POPPA"—NOTORIOUS B.I.G.

"U.N.I.T.Y."—QUEEN LATIFA

"NOTHIN' BUT A G THANG"—DR. DRE & SNOOP DOGGY DOG

"HARD KNOCK LIFE"—JAY-Z

"I GOT A MAN"—POSITIVE K

"IN DA CLUB"—50 CENT

"I USED TO LOVE H.E.R."—COMMON

"HATE ME NOW"—NAS FEATURING DIDDY

"SOUTH BRONX"—KRS ONE

Hip Hop Hooray

Four

Rock Da House Interviews

Interview with Michael Holman

Q. "Graffiti Rock" was way ahead of its time. What did you sense about Hip-Hop at that time that lead you to create "Graffiti Rock"?

A. What I was seeing in the world of Hip-Hop at the stage, we're talking about the term "Hip-Hop" wasn't even used, but I could see, as a resident and an artist and musician, on the downtown art scene looking around me and seeing in New York City all the things in the Bronx, I thought that I was witnessing the birth of a new form of sub-culture like Rock-N-Roll or Jazz where Rock-N-Roll had it's music, it's own look, had it's own fashion, had it's own literature and syntax, had it's own dances; the same with Jazz. I was seeing that with what later on became Hip-Hop.

There's this incredible dance form, break dancing or b-boying, that is so acrobatic and so entertaining—such a spectacle, if you will. People, whenever they see it, they stop and stare, whether it's on the streets, Time Square, or whether it's at the clubs. The music, often times Hip-Hop, deejays were playing were ten years or more older from another period, even before disco. Nevertheless, the kids were looking back at their parents record collection and digging out the best of James Brown, Jimmy Castor Bunch, songs like "The Mexican" and "Apache" for the dancer and everyone involved were wearing certain fashions.

And then there were the emcees on the microphone making the party go.

And there was a political or social party component in that all of these artists were coming together in a friendly benign way to find a way to stop the fighting that was going on between the gangs in New York. So there was a sociological/political edge to it and it was all coming out of one place and it seemed so regional and it was all coming from Blacks and Latinos in New York City. So, to me, it was screaming that this was a scene that other people were going to tap into and want to identify with that was going to inspire other people, other races, other socio-economic backgrounds, and I could see it. There was no effort putting it into a cohesive movement. It was already doing this on its own. It had a ground swell and a natural flow.

"Graffiti Rock," I would have to say, is the first major presentation of Hip-Hop in national entertainment media.

Q. The battle on "Graffiti Rock" between Kool Moe Dee and Special K against Run- DMC; Was it staged or was it real?

A. It was a little bit of both. It was something that we knew we would do. I think the reason we did the battle the way we did it is because Run-DMC really didn't know how to battle like the Treacherous Three knew how to battle. It would've been kind of lopsided so we kind of made it staged. Nothing against Run-DMC, but they blew up kind of fast and I don't think they went through the same challenges the Treacherous Three did in terms of battling. I think that they were super talented emcees, but if they had to battle toe to toe with Special K and Kool Moe Dee, they would've gotten slaughtered and for that reason, we kind of made it staged.

Q. What is your greatest moment in Hip-Hop?

A. I befriended Malcolm McClaren, who was the manager of the Sex Pistols, which Punk Rock was another heavy movement

I got to be a part of, and Malcolm McClaren was a big hero of mine and I was introduced to him as I was in the middle of my impresario role in the early days of Hip-Hop and I had the opportunity to introduce him to Hip-Hop. I brought him uptown with another RCA Executive, Rory Johnson, to a Bambaataa throw down and exposed him to all things Hip-Hop. He was so excited about it, he asked me to put together a review of all the different artists I had already been working with for the last couple of years to open up for his band the Bow Wow Wow at the Ritz down in downtown Manhattan.

I got Bambaataa on the turntables, Jazzy Jay on the turntables, emcees on the mic, the Rock Steady Crew b-boying. We had graffiti—I had, like, a whole Hip-Hop review and, in my opinion, this was the first time that anyone had ever put together all the elements of Hip-Hop and presented it to a mass audience—a live audience. This young lady who had gone to see Bow Wow Wow saw my show. She had a night at this club called the grill on 2nd Avenue and the manager of the Clash, his name was Cosmo, it was his night and he just gave it to her, Thursday night. She approached me and said, "What do you think about bringing your whole review to my club, the Grill, and we make it like a nightclub act?"

I said, "Yeah! That was really great!" and I had Phase II to do the fliers. I had Ramellzee do all kinds of three-dimensional graffiti statues, sculptures. I had Fab 5 Freddy on the mic. I had Kool Herc, I had Bambaataa, Jazzy Jay, the Rock Steady Crew dancing, and I invited all of my friends from the downtown scene as well as the downtown press/media. I believe it was the first time that all the elements of Hip-Hop were brought together as a movement under one roof. I have to say that putting together my Hip-Hop review at the Grill was the highlight of my Hip-Hop experience, bringing the New York Times and all the national and international media, newspapers, and magazines to come and write about it and start spreading it out to other parts of the city, country, and world.

Q. Is Hip-Hop dead?

A. Unfortunately, I think that Rap has stolen the term "Hip-Hop" from the culture. I do not believe that Rap is Hip-Hop. It's one element of Hip-Hop. Back when that move was made of stealing the term Hip-Hop and applying it to Rap to the exclusion of b-boying, turntablism, deejaying, fashion, and graffiti, Hip-Hop died. At the exclusion of the other disciplines, Rap, in a way, killed Hip-Hop, which was done back in the 90s. The other elements didn't die, but Hip-Hop as a cohesive culture died when all of its facets separated from each other and went on their own. So Hip-Hop is dead.

My greatest moment in Hip-Hop was asking Kool Herc if I can rock the mic at one of his jams and seeing Hip-Hop move from the parks and jams to the Roxy in Manhattan.

—Donald D

Interview with Sal Abbatiello

Q. How would you describe your legacy in Hip-Hop?

A. I was probably the first one to play a Rap record because there wasn't any Rap clubs, there were no radio stations, so the only venues you could really go to were either Harlem or give it to the street deejay, but I was the only commercial place where people would be able to hear it. I broke most of the records in *The Fever*. Kurtis Blow was the first one to give me a gold record 'cause I was probably the first one to play "Christmas Rhymes." When their [Sugarhill Gang] record went double-platinum, I was the first one to play "Rapper's Delight" in New York, so they gave me the record in being instrumental in helping them go double-platinum.

My father had a bar on 167th Street called Pepper and Salt and he was going to open a club called Disco Fever for an older R&B crowd. This was in 1976, so I go to the club hanging out and this guy, Sweet G, and when the deejay would go home early, he [Sweet G] would wait around to get on the turntables. So when he got on, it was like 4:00 AM, 4:30 AM and my father didn't mind, so when G got on, he would do nursery rhymes and I was sitting there drinking and listening saying, "What the hell?" Everybody started telling me that's what was going on in the Bronx; People are talking over the music.

I started hanging out, investigating, going to the parks. I went to see Kool Herc at a club and then I went to the park and started hearing names like Love Bug Starski, Eddie Cheba, Pete DJ Jones, Grandmaster Flash, but the one I kept hearing about was Grandmaster Flash. So I went to see him and I saw the reaction from the crowd and I was like, "Holy shit! It's amazing what they're doing!" So I went to my father and said, "I think I fell upon something." So I'm trying to convince my father to do it and all his friends are telling him, "No, don't bring that shit in here, man; a bunch of noise; a bunch of fucking hoodlums." I'm trying to bring entertainment to the club, so I bring in two or three disco acts in the club and they're all flopping.

Finally, I convince him to give me a Tuesday night—what could happen? So finally, he said, "Yes!" I go to Flash. Now I got to convince Flash to come into a club. Flash is used to doing these one-nighters at the Audubon and Savoy Manner and all these big catering clubs and he's getting a little extra money. So I'm trying to convince him to come to this club and that he'll get famous there plus he'll be there on a weekly basis and he'll get discovered there. I'm offering him like $75.00 to deejay. He goes, "I got all of these rappers!" and I go, "Look, $75.00 for you and all the five rappers and that's it. If you want to become famous, you come to the place." So I convince him to play opening night Tuesday and 600 people show up. It was out of control.

There was another club back in the day called 371. 371 was on 167th Street also, except I was all the way on the East side and they were all the way on the West side. 371 catered more to Nicky Barnes, the classy R&B, older, drug crowd; hustler, fly guy, pimp, and shit like that and D.J. Hollywood was over there. Hollywood had a deejay called D.J. June Bug who was Puerto Rican and he was the first famous Latino deejay. I go after June Bug. Now, Tuesdays are going so good. I tell my father, "Let's do another night." So I find Luv Bug Starski and we do Monday night.

Now Mondays are packed! Now Sweet G starts deejaying on Friday and Saturday until I brought in June Bug. Now June Bug is the house deejay on the weekends, I promoted Sweet G as the host emcee, and I'm the General Manager. D.J. Hollywood, after two years, came on Wednesday, Eddie Cheeba was on Sunday, we brought Reggie Wells in on a Thursday, and then we opened up another room downstairs and then we brought in Star Child and Brucie B. It was all from there and then records started getting made in '79 and we became the Hip-Hop capitol of the world.

I started the Rucker's league in 1979, which was the same year "Rapper's Delight" came out. The first game of the Entertainment Basketball League, which I started with Mr. Magic and Greg from the Disco 4, was Disco Fever against Sugarhill Records and 3,000 people showed up for the game at Morris Park. In 1983, Disco Fever was the Mecca of Hip-Hop. Sometimes I would have 30 recording artists in my club (Disco Fever) at the same time. That was unheard of. Unprecedented. I don't think that ever happened in the history of music except for maybe Studio 54, and I still don't think that many people would be in Studio 54 at the same time, in the same night.

Interview with Grandmaster Mele Mel

Q. What are your three favorite songs that you recorded?

A. "White Lines," "The Message," and "Vice" from the *Miami Vice* soundtrack.

Q. How do you feel about Rap music today?

A. Right now, it's more based on image than music. It's counterproductive because they're not really selling music.

Q. Do you feel the original artists or pioneers receive the recognition they deserve?

A. Oh yeah, we receive the recognition. Everybody knows us and what we did for Hip-Hop, so I would say we do get the recognition. However, we get the recognition, but we don't get the respect and that's basically for all the pioneers. We didn't have the opportunity to be successful in the record business as our counterparts. We didn't make the kind of money back then the way guys are making money today just like the Temptations didn't make the kind of money Jodeci made.

Q. Big Guns Entertainment, can you tell me about that?

A. Big Guns Entertainment is not just a record label, it's a fitness program and we're writing a book and going to have a college lecture tour. Big Guns Entertainment is everything Mele Mel. Our (old school) position in the industry is marginalized and minimized and that's why I created Big Guns and it's successful, very successful. It has to be marketed in the right way. I may not make the kind of money that a Jay-Z or Diddy might make, but I don't need money to be successful. This is what a lot of cats out there don't understand. They think the music business is like selling drugs, but you don't sell drugs, the drugs sell themselves, you just pass it along to the junkies to get high and that's how a lot of them think the music business is like, but it's not. It's different. You have to know how to market what you're selling. That's why Big Guns Entertainment will be successful.

Q. What is your greatest moment in Hip-Hop?

A. My greatest moment in Hip-Hop, I would have to say, is when I performed at the Grammys with Chaka Khan for the song, "I Feel For You." The song won a Grammy Award for Record of the Year and an American Music Award and went platinum.

My greatest moment in Hip-Hop is when me and Roxanne Shanté battled in Raleigh, North Carolina at the Dome. For the first time, (5,000) seats sold out and we went for ours—history!

—Sparky D

Interview with Kurtis Blow

Q. You got started back in the mid-to-late 70s with Russell Simmons as your manager. How did you meet Russell?

A. At first, Russell and I were college buddies at City College in New York. I introduced him to Hip-Hop, actually. It was a crazy story that happened. When I was in high school, I had this thing where I wanted to become a deejay. I was at the High School of Music and Arts at the college campus over there in Harlem, but we used to go to the parties over at the college. They had a little rec. room over there and that's where I met Russell.

When I saw him, I said, "Man! You look like this cat that used to go to this club called Mel Guinn with Pete D.J. Jones! I used to see you do the Brooklyn Hustle! Is that you?" And he said, "Yeah, yeah. That's me." I introduced myself to him, telling him, "I'm a deejay, I'm coming to the college, and I'm going to major in communications and I want you to introduce me to Reggie Wells." He was a hot deejay at the time. So, I told Russell, "I'm in the 11th grade right now. It's going to take me two years before I get into the college. Will you introduce me then?" And he was like, "Alright young kid. Alright."

I ended up graduating a year early and jumped into CCNY a year early. The next year, I was on the campus. I saw Russell at registration day and I was like, "Yo, yo! What's up Russell? I told you I was coming, but I made it a year early man!" He said, "Wow, you're real serious," and we became buddies. He introduced me to everybody and we became partners. He actually helped me get my record deal and then after that, I made him my manager. We were partners, but we used to fight from time-to-time because we didn't always see eye-to-eye.

Q. At one point, you worked with Grandmaster Flash and you all were the Furious 6?

A. Yeah, at one point, I had met Flash up at the 371 Club. I was looking for a deejay at that time. Flash was looking for an emcee and he was like, "I need an emcee. Can you come and emcee for me?" So I got down with Flash and we were rocking for a while. Then Mele Mel came around and it was Kurtis Blow and Mele Mel. Wow! Mele Mel and I was partners for maybe a year and then all the Furious came back and they put me down. I was actually the 7th member. The 6th emcee was a guy I went to the School of Music and Arts with. His name was Kool Kyle (The Star Child). Grandmaster Flash and the Furious 7—we were like the Earth, Wind and Fire of Hip-Hop.

Q. How did you get involved with Holy Hip-Hop?

A. Holy Hip-Hop was a gradual thing. It happened in the Bronx. I went to a church function because they wanted to honor old school Hip-Hop. So me, Grandmaster Caz, Waterbed Kev, and Raheim went over there. They were a great crowd, very nice to us. They had Christian rappers there doing their thing. Afterwards, I went to the Pastor and said, "This is a great, great thing. You all need to do this every week." And he said, "Wow! Maybe you're right. What would you want to call it?" Kurtis and I said, "Call it the Hip-Hop Church."

Q. What impact do you think *Krush Groove* had on mainstream America?

A. I think all of the movies at that time had an impact. *Wild Style* was an incredible raw film on Hip-Hop. Then you had *Beat Street* and then *Breakin'*. *Breakin'* sold a lot of tickets in the theatres and then *Krush Groove* was very hot. It was me, Run-DMC, the Fat Boys, New Edition, and Sheila E. It was a hot,

hot movie with a lot of stars in it. We really acted very, very well and I give the props out to Gloria Shultz, who was the wife of Michael Shultz, the Director. She went over the script with us and actually tutored us on the set. We had no acting experience. It was pure raw talent.

Q. What would be the number one thing you love about Hip-Hop today?

A. One thing I love about Hip-Hop is that it's more than just an industry, it is really a culture. Until you really live it like I have lived it, you wouldn't understand it. It's been a part of my life, not just the music that I listen to, not just the way I dance, not just the graffiti art I love to look at. It's a way of life. It's in your heart.

Q. What would be the one thing you dislike about Hip-Hop today?

A. Let me give you two things. When the emcee is on the mic. and I've been saying this since 1978 when I learned how to project my vocals from the diaphragm, which gives you power, which most emcees do not do, and two, don't clutch the microphone. You sound horrible on stage. The other thing is, and I always say this as an analogy, Hip-Hop is like the mother of four children who are like the elements—rapping, breaking, deejaying and graffiti art. If one of the children becomes successful, should that child forget about his brothers or should that child go back to his brothers and help them?

Q. How will you like for Hip-Hop to remember Kurtis Blow?

A. A true pioneer who blazed the trail for Hip-Hop and a man of God. A man of God first.

Hall of Fame Hits

"ONE FOR THE TREBLE"—DAVY D.M.X.

"WHATEVER YOU LIKE"—T.I.

"NEW YORK, NEW YORK"—GRAND MASTER FLASH & THE FURIOUS 5

"RUFF NECK"—M.C. LYTE

"KEEP YA HEAD UP"—2 PAC

"LOSE YOURSELF"—EMINEM

"FLAVA IN YA EAR"—CRAIG MAC

"C'MON N RIDE IT (THE TRAIN)"—QUAD CITY DJ'S

"NEW JACK SWING"—WRECKS-N-EFFECT

"WHOOP THERE IT IS"—TAG TEAM

"MY ADIDAS"—RUN-DMC

"GANGSTER'S PARADISE"—COOLIO

"THE CHOICE IS YOURS"—BLACK SHEEP

"ON THE SMOOTH TIP"—SWEET TEE

"CINDERFELLA DANA DANE"—DANA DANE

Hip Hop Hooray

Five

Flash Back 1986

In the news, the U.S. Supreme Court reaffirmed abortion rights; The Chicago Bears won the Super Bowl; and Chicago Bulls' star Michael Jordan set an NBA record scoring 63 points in a playoff game. The Oprah Winfrey Show hit national television for the first time and the New York Mets won the World Series. Nintendo games were introduced and the movie *Platoon* was a hit in the theaters. The Boston Celtics, led by Larry Bird, defeated the Los Angeles Lakers to win the NBA championship.

1986 was a stellar year in Hip-Hop. This was the beginning of what is commonly referred to as the Golden Era. Run-DMC dropped their new LP *Raising Hell* and their first single, "My Adidas" raced up the music charts. Their next single, "Walk This Way," a collaborated remake with the Rock group Aerosmith, took them over the top and off the charts. Once they crossed over to the Pop charts, Run-DMC became synonymous with Rap music.

Raising Hell became the biggest selling Rap album of all time, surpassing the three million sales mark and the became first Rap album to hit #1 on the Billboard R&B/Hip-Hop chart. Riding the success of the album, Run DMC became the first Rap act to have a music video aired on MTV and the first to perform on the popular TV show *American Bandstand*. They graced the cover of *Rolling Stone Magazine* and received a Grammy Award nomination.

Aside from the success of Run DMC, a number of Rap artists hit the scene. The dynamic duo of Eric B and Rakim smoked the streets with their debut cut, "Eric B is President" b/w My Melody. KRS-One and Boogie Down Productions hit with "South Bronx" and Salt 'N Pepa, the first female Rap act to impact the game since Sequence, scored with "My Mic. Sounds Nice." Heavy D and the Boyz dropped "Mr. Big Stuff" and rocked the radio airwaves for weeks and West coast phenom Ice Tee hit hard with "6 In the Morning."

Whistle scored a hit with "Just Buggin'," Ultramagnetic MCs dropped "Ego Trippin'" and Just Ice rocked with "Back to the Old School." Legendary rapper Kool Moe Dee of Treacherous Three fame rocked the streets with "Go See the Doctor," a comical Rap about a sexually transmitted disease. The song was produced by a teenaged Teddy Riley. Timex Social Club scored a hit with "Rumors" and the Real Roxanne hit big with "Howie's Tee'd Off." Joeski Love set it off with his smash hit "Peewee's Dance," based on the character from the popular movie.

Grandmaster Flash made a return with a new group and scored a popular cut with "Style." Dougie Fresh and the Get Fresh Crew climbed the charts with "All the Way To Heaven" and Steady B, from out of Philadelphia, dropped "Bring The Beat Back." Grandmaster Caz of the legendary Cold Crush Brothers won the New Music Seminar's Rap contest for the title of World Supremacy and Mele Mel became the first Rap artist to win an Emmy Award for an anti-drug Rap commercial aired on WNBC in New York.

Whodini climbed the charts with their platinum single "Funky Beat" and followed it up with the mega hit "One Love" from their *Back In Black* LP. The Fat Boys returned with "Big and Beautiful" and DJ Jazzy Jeff and the Fresh Prince debuted with the single "Girls of the World Ain't Nothin' But Trouble," set to the theme music of the 1960s popular television show *I Dream of Jeannie*. The Boogie Boys made noise with "Girl Talk" and Biz Markie rocked the streets with "Play The Music With Your Mouth Biz," a song in which he demonstrated his beat box skills. The Beastie Boys dropped "License To Ill,"

Flash Back 1986

becoming the first Rap album to reach number one on the Billboard album chart, surpassing Run DMC in album sales and popularity.

Just Ice dropped "Latoya" and "Cold Getting' Dumb" while Sweet Tee and Jazzy Joyce scored with "It's My Beat." Cut Master DC rocked the underground hit "Brooklyn Rocks the Best" and the Real Roxanne rode the charts with "Bang Zoom (Let's Go-Go)." One of the most significant moments in Hip-Hop was the song "King Holiday" by The King Dream Choir and Holiday Crew, a collaboration of artists that included: El DeBarge, Full Force, Grandmaster Mele Mel, Whitney Houston, Kurtis Blow, Stacy Lattisaw, Lisa Lisa, Teena Marie, Menudo, Stephanie Mills, New Edition, Run DMC, James "JT" Taylor, and Whodini.

My greatest moment in Hip-Hop was the release of 'The Adventures of Super Rhymes' and the world accepted it with open arms.

—Jimmy Spicer

Heavy Waters

Naked and shackled weaken and weary
300 feet dragging chains on board
Faces full of fear and hearts full of fury
Went down to the bottom as the ocean roared
A room of steamy heat and cluttering sounds
Of moans and groans and cries filled the air
In utter darkness, a stench surrounds
The enduring pains they could no longer bare
The ship took sail as they lay on the planking
With lingering thoughts of confusion and death
Rattling sounds of chains that were clanking
Muffled prayers said under their breath
With the rush of the waters, the shipped moved and turned
Boards would rub up against their flesh
'Til their skin wore down to the bone and burned
So day after day their wounds stayed fresh
They banged the iron cuffs that was on their wrist
Until total exhaustion made them collapse
And their eyes were filled with a watery mist
Wondering if they'll ever get out the steel traps
They found themselves locked down in a flood
Of nothing but urine and waste all around
The whole floor was covered with vomit and blood
And lifeless bodies still shackled and bound
The ones found dead were taken up and dumped
Thrown overboard with the rest of the trash
The ones that revolted gave up and jumped
Became shark food by the time they'd splash
After endless weeks, the ship reached land
And the ones that survived struggled to the dock
Broken down with sickness and could barely stand
A hundred feet dragging chains to the auction block

Flash Back 1986

The Raising Hell Tour (1987)

Featuring Run-DMC—Whodini—L.L. Cool J

May 24 Atlanta, GA
The Omni

May 25 Nashville, TN
Municipal Auditorium

May 28 Albuquerque, NM
Kinsley Coliseum

May 29 Phoenix, AZ
Coliseum

May 30 Los Angeles, CA
L.A. Sportatorium

June 6 Birmingham, AL
Civic Center

June 7 Memphis, TN
Mid-South Coliseum

June 15 Dallas, TX
Reunion Arena

June 20 Greensboro, NC
Greensboro Coliseum

June 21 Philadelphia, PA
Spectrum

June 25 Saginaw, MI
Wendler Arena

June 26 Cleveland, Ohio
Public Hall

June 27 Baltimore, MD
Civic Center

June 28 Pittsburgh, PA
Civic Center

June 29 Rochester, NY
Civic Center

July 2 Milwaukee, WI
The Mecca

July 5 Detroit, MI
Joe Louis Arena

July 6 Chicago, IL
The Pavilion

July 12 Jacksonville, FL
Veterans Memorial

July 13 New Orleans, LA
University of New Orleans

July 19 New York, NY
Madison Square Garden

"My greatest moment in Hip-Hop, that would be having a #1 Hip-Hop single on the Billboard Hip-Hop Chart three times in a row by the same artist, same album. Yes Sir."
—"Hit Man" Howie Tee

Six

The Funky Fresh Era

King Holiday

One of the most significant moments in Hip-Hop took place in 1986. Dexter King, son of slain Civil Rights leader Dr. Martin Luther King Jr., spearheaded the King Holiday project as a tribute in honor of his father's Holiday. Melle Mel was recruited as one of the principal lyricist and vocalists for the song "King Holiday" that included a number of superstar artists called the King Dream Chorus which consisted of: El DeBarge, Full Force, Grandmaster Mele Mel, Whitney Houston, Kurtis Blow, Stacy Lattisaw, Lisa Lisa, Teena Marie, Menudo, Stephanie Mills, New Edition, Run-DMC, James "JT" Taylor, and Whodini.

This was the first collaboration of Rap artists and their participation in honoring one of America's greatest heroes is not only a timeless event, but memorable beyond words. "He had a dream, now it's up to you to see it through, to make it come true!"

Fresh Fest

In 1984, the *Fresh Fest* became Hip-Hop's first national tour. The *Fresh Fest* was originally scheduled for a 30-city tour date and featured such acts as Kurtis Blow performing hits like "The Breaks," "Party Time," and "Basketball;" Run-DMC performed "Sucker MC's," "It's Like That," and "Rock Box;" The Fat Boys performed "Fat Boys" and "Jail House Rap;" Whodini performed their big hits "Five Minutes of

Funk," "Friends," "Big Mouth," and "Freaks Come Out At Night;" and Newcleus performed "Jam On Revenge." Sponsored by Swatch Watch, the *Fresh Fest* rocked shows with over 400,000 people in sold-out performances across the country.

Who We Rolling With?

By 1985, Rush Productions, located in lower Manhattan, became the first powerhouse management company in the Rap game. Headed by Russell Simmons, Rush had an all-star lineup that included Kurtis Blow, Whodini, Run-DMC, Dr. Jeckyl and Mr. Hyde, Sweet G, and Spyder D. They were some of the most popular Rap acts around and their songs dominated the radio airwaves and Rap charts. Sponsoring Rap tours around the country and other events, Rush Productions played a major role in the mainstream development of Hip-Hop. In fact, on Eric B and Rakim's classic 1987 hit "Paid In Full," in between the funky grooves of the thick bass lines, the question was asked, "So, who we rollin' with?" And the response was, "We rollin' with Rush."

I'm The New Fool In Town

Digital Underground hit the Rap scene in 1987, but didn't gain momentum until their hit song "Dowutchyalike" was released in 1989. Members Shock G and Chopmaster J founded the group, based out of Oakland, California. What made them unique outside of their outrageous costumes and odd, eclectic rhyme styles were their alter-egos. Humpty Hump, in particular, with the fake nose, goofy-looking glasses and comical voice, a character created by Shock G, is what made their song "The Humpty Dance" a classic and the group a household name.

As Nasty As They Wanna Be

In 1989, Luther "Luke" Campbell and the 2 Live Crew made music history. Their album *As Nasty As They Wanna Be* became the first record ever to be classified as 'obscene' by a US Court. Nevertheless, the controversy surrounding the LP from Freedom of Speech to Parental Advisory Warnings generated the media hype that pushed their record sales to double-platinum status and spawned the hit single "Me So Horny." What added fuel to the fire was a show overseas. While Luke performed, a female from the audience walked on stage and, to the utter disbelief of thousands in attendance, she began performing oral copulation on the artist.

Wild Thing

Tone-Loc, known for his deep and raspy voice, was virtually an unknown emcee that crashed into the Rap game with the triple-platinum single "Wild Thing" in 1989. His follow-up single "Funky Cold Medina" was just as popular of a hit, which elevated his status as a rising Rap superstar. After releasing the two mega-hit singles, Tone dropped his debut LP *Loc'ed After Dark* and it became the second Rap album ever to top the Pop charts.

How Ya Like Me Now

The NAACP Image Awards celebrates the outstanding achievements and performances of people of color in performing arts. As a tribute to the best in the world of entertainment, the NAACP honored Kool Moe Dee as the first Rap artist to receive the prestigious award in 1988. The award came on the heels of Kool Moe Dee's success with the platinum album "How Ya Like Me Now" which featured hits from the title cut and "Wild, Wild West," a song addressing the dangers of gun violence and Black-on-Black crime.

Sun City

In 1985, E Street Band guitarist Steven Van Zandt decided to take a couple of trips to South Africa to learn about the injustices of the White South African Government. His visits to the area of Botswana allowed him to witness the devastation of racial injustice first hand and it motivated him to write the song "Sun City," the name the region is often referred to. The song was a protest for musical artists not to play in South Africa. Co-produced by Arthur Baker, the song enlisted the talents of 51 acts, which included Afrika Bambaataa, Kurtis Blow, Grandmaster Melle Mel, Scorpio, the Fat Boys, and Run-DMC.

Excuse Me Doug E Fresh

Most people first heard of the human beat box in 1983 on the Fat Boys' hit songs. However, in 1985, Doug E Fresh and the Get Fresh Crew released the song "The Show" and once it hit the airwaves, it challenged the mainstream perception and created controversy as to who created the human beat box. "The Show" was a huge hit and in the song, Doug E Fresh insists that he invented the beat box and displays exemplary skills throughout the record and on the b-side hit "La Di Da Di." Doug admits that he created the beat box by accident while performing when the sound system went out. He improvised by attempting to imitate the drum machine and the crowd went wild.

Escape

In 1984, Rap group Whodini released their second LP on Jive Records. The album was titled *Escape*, a follow-up to their self-titled debut album that featured the hits, "Magic's Wand" and "Haunted House of Rock." *Escape*, however, would take them to another level with the success of their first single, "Five Minutes Of Funk" and the mega-hit "Friends." Additionally, the LP spawned the hits "Big Mouth" and the classic joint "Freaks Come Out At Night." *Escape* became the first Rap album to be certified platinum.

FOCUS

Right On! Magazine released its first copy of *FOCUS*, a special publication dedicated to Rap music, in the winter of 1983. The front cover featured Kurtis Blow, Grandmaster Flash, and the Furious Five and comedian/actor Eddie Murphy who ironically released a Rap song on his self-titled debut album. In addition to their articles were write-ups on the Fearless Four, The Sugarhill Gang, the West Street Mob, and break-dancing. *FOCUS* was the blueprint for the popular Hip-Hop magazines today such as *The Source*, *XXL*, *Rap Pages*, and *Vibe*, among others.

The Funky Fresh Era

Back on the Block

One of the most notable events in 1989 was *Back On the Block* by Quincy Jones. Q put together a star-studded cast of artists, including musical greats such as Ella Fitzgerald, Miles Davis, Sarah Vaughn, Dizzy Gillespie, and Ray Charles, to name a few. He added the Hip-Hop equivalent with Ice T, Grandmaster Melle Mel, Big Daddy Kane, and Kool Moe Dee. The Hip-Hop contribution helped to secure the albums' platinum status and Grammy Awards en route to becoming one of the greatest jazz albums ever made.

Self Destruction

In 1989, Stop the Movement was founded by KRS-One. The movement was signified with the song "Self-Destruction" and was spearheaded by the Teacha. A collaboration of emcees came together to include Just Ice, MC Lyte, Heavy D, Stet emcees Chuck D and Flavor Flav from Public Enemy, Ms. Melody, Doug E. Fresh, and Kool Moe Dee. The song addressed the growing violence in the Hip-Hop and Black community and left most of us amazed with Moe Dee's rhyme "I never ever ran from the Ku Klux Klan and I shouldn't have to run from a Black man."

The Source

David Mays and Jon Shecter founded *The Source* magazine in 1988. Originally a newsletter on the college campus of Harvard University, *The Source* became the most popular Hip-Hop magazine by the early 90s. Featuring the biggest Rap stars on the front cover like Ice Cube, KRS-One, Dr. Dre, and Busta Rhymes, the magazine's popularity became unparalleled in the world of journalism. The success of its monthly issues led to an annual awards show, The Source Awards, honoring artists for their achievements in Hip-Hop. The magazine spawned a number of competitors from *Rap Pages* to *Vibe*, but still remains as one of the premier Rap magazines on the market.

Who's Da' Goat?

Rhymes hit like a semi-automatic
Acrobatic
Flipping styles like balance beams
Even more dramatic
Than a scene from "Fast
And the Furious" non-stop
I go all out
And do it all as I drop
Mad skills leaving steel
With rust and corrosion
And getting cream
Like an explosion in a Trojan
First I smoke the mic.
And leave it in an ashtray
Poetic like Maya
With enough style to sashay
As I write with a pen
That a hand grenade is missin'
Wires catch fire
Mic. shorts and speakers hissin'
Everything beneath the cranium
Is deep as uranium
As I stick to the drum
Like gum whether a stadium,
Block party, schoolyard,
Or back in the park
And after it smokes
The mic. will spark in the dark
And if you wanna know
Who could write such a rhyme
XLG
Who's the greatest of all time?

Seven

Throw Your Hands Up In the Air Interviews

Interview with Sweet Tee

Q. Who were the artists that influenced you when you were coming up in Hip-Hop?

A. Well, because I came out, like, in the beginning, there weren't any Rap artists that influenced me. You know, my very first record was with Davy DMX, "One for the Treble," right at the beginning. There weren't Rap artists for me to say who were my inspirations. I started rhyming when deejays were playing in the parks, so I had to be on my A-game to go against whoever it was. That was my inspiration in the beginning.

Q. As an emcee, do you think that female artists get the recognition that they deserve?

A. I think there's room for females, but you have to find your way. Be real with what you're doing and do it. I never really felt that girls were being held back. I felt, if anything, it was easier for me.

Q. How do you feel about Hip-Hop today?

A. I love it. I like the music, but I can say, on a general note, some of it is kind of repetitive and that scares me. Some of it sounds like the same thing. I like the feel of the music. You know, I've done a lot of traveling over the last year going to different states and I'm happy to see that rappers are like business men and the business is able to get to that point like what we did was not in vain. We made a serious notch—maybe not with millions of dollars, but I helped it get there. I remember when people said it was a fad and that it wasn't going to last, so I'm proud to see it grow to where it is. It is a way of life all over the world.

Q. What are your thoughts about how emcees battled back in the day as opposed to what is considered a battle in today's market?

A. I think the battle CDs, they go at it like how we did, you know? They do what they got to do, but, you know, it's about music now, so you want to sound hot with everything you're saying, but if you don't have a hot hook, then it's not a good record and it feels like you don't win that way. I think it changed a little bit because now you need that hook.

Q. What current projects are you working on?

A. I started going to the studio a little while ago and I'm working on a CD. This Spring, I'm going to drop a couple of singles. I know the music business is really different than it was and it might be in my best interest that the music business is the way it is. It's not like back when you signed with a label and you have to wait and then the schedule—you don't have to do that now. I got some hot records so far and I'm going to put it out there.

Q. What is your greatest moment in Hip-Hop?

A. It's funny because it's the same thing Latifah spoke about me in her book; the same pivotal moment for her was the pivotal moment for me. Me and Jazzy Joyce were performing at the Latin Quarters and we pulled up in a limousine and there was a line all the way down the block and the marquee wasn't on. Our names were on there, but the marquee was off and we were like, "What's going on? Are they closed? Why won't they let anybody in?" We stop the limousine and I'm like, "Let me find out what happened." So Herby goes in and he comes back out and he said, "Okay, the place is at capacity and that's why the marquee is off." That was one of the nights that I was in shock, like, I've done a lot of things—I did Soul Train and other stuff, but this particular night was crazy! We went inside and just did it and the Latin Quarters called us because they had to have us back again for another show.

Music is just like any other business when it comes to success. Fast food chains are more popular and make a lot more money than five star restaurants, just like some rappers that are mediocre in terms of skill sell more records and make bigger hits than some of the best MCs in the history of the game. When I look at a combination of subject matter, versatility, and lyrics, Sean XLG is untouchable and, in my opinion, he's the greatest rapper of all time.
—DJ Money

Dana Dane

Q. Who influenced you in Hip-Hop?

A. Well, you know, back in the day, the first record they had on wax was 1979 and even before that you had brothers on the street rocking cassette tapes. You had Treacherous Three and Cold Crush Brothers, Afrika Bambaataa, Fearless Four, Crash Crew, all those groups early on who I listened to on cassette tapes and boom boxes.

Q. How did you meet Slick Rick and form the Kangol Krew?

A. The Kangol Krew, that was a high school group. The four of us were in classes together. We never recorded anything actually; just did our thing in the lunchroom cafeteria.

Q. Between you and Slick Rick, which one of you guys invented the English accent for your rhymes?

A. I can't really say either one of us invented it. You know, Rick is originally from Jamaica. The other cats in the group had a Reggae background as well. I would have to say the sound was created by all of us. I can't take any credit for it, but I don't think either one of us can take credit for it. If anybody can take credit for it, I would have to give it to Lance Brown and Slick Rick because they were Jamaican.

Q. There's a science to storytelling that a lot of people don't understand. Can you explain some of the details that go into it?

A. My perspective, I've always dealt from writing my stories in chronological order from introduction to body to conclusion. I do it basically like you would do a short story. Some people delve into telling stories, but they jump everywhere and, to me, that doesn't really work. You have to be able to capture people's imagination where they can see your words and, hopefully, travel with you without ever having a video or a picture to show them. A lot of emcees early on liked to follow a certain format, a certain idea. If a song was called a message, they made sure that the lyrics followed the message. If the song was about criminal-minded, it was about the criminal-minded idea of it. If it was a children's story, it was children's story. Now-a-days, with some of them, as long as their words Rap together and the last two bars say what the hook is, they think they created something formatted, but it's really more abstract these days.

Q. What is one thing about you that most people don't know?

A. A. I wrote half of my album on the road with Whodini. This is a story I always tell. I had "Nightmares" out and I went to Madison Square Garden and I went backstage. It was Run-DMC, Whodini, Beastie Boys, and L.L. Cool J. I met Grandmaster Dee and three days later, I'm on a tour bus with them and we're touring the nation. I wrote a lot of *Dana Dane with Fame* on their tour bus.

Q. Do you think storytelling is a dying art form in today's music?

A. Yeah, I don't think that kids today recognize and respect the craft of it. Biggie was one of the last great storytellers and we do have Eminem. Biggie was really a phenomenal storywriter and, I would say, he would give Slick Rick and myself a run for his money on any day. That's probably why he was considered the greatest rapper of all time because not only did he have his abstract rhymes, but he had story rhymes and the visuals of how he put it down was like none other, other than Slick Rick, myself, and the Kangol Krew. Dana Dane has dealt with it, Nas has dealt with it, and Jay-Z has the talent to do it, but cats today, it's a whole bunch of rhyming, but no stories.

Q. Is Hip-Hop dead?

A. That was just something to get people to pay attention. You know Hip-Hop was spiraling downward, everybody was doing the same thing, nobody was taking responsibility for what they were doing in Hip-Hop, and it was just going around in circles and the circle was going down. I think, sooner or later, someone had to step up say something about Hip-Hop and I think that was the perfect avenue for people to talk about what Hip-Hop was so younger generations can recognize what Hip-Hop was. And from that conversation, we, as classical Hip-Hop artists, were no longer old school and played out. Now, we became old school and respected. It was a time where a lot of pioneering Hip-Hop heads were bitter because they weren't getting the proper respect that they were due and after a while, they started saying, "You know what? We know what we did for the game, so were going to keep moving forward." Nas put that language out there and testing people's Hip-Hop knowledge. So, is Hip-Hop dead? No, Hip-Hop isn't dead because I know where it came from.

Q. What is your greatest moment in Hip-Hop?

A. I thought about it last night and, as I look back on my career, I was the first Brooklyn, Hip-Hop, solo emcee to go gold and probably the fourth solo Hip-Hop artist to go gold: Kurtis Blow, L.L., and Kool Mo Dee. Other than that, it was me. That was probably my greatest accomplishment. *Dana Dane with Fame* went gold in 1987.

Q. Are there any projects you're working on we can look forward to?

A. Actually, February 24, 2009, my debut novel under Nikki Turner Presents *Numbers* by Dana Dane will be released by Random House. My son, Young Dane, wants to get into the music business, so what I'm going to do is create a soundtrack for the book and I'll probably do about 8 to 10 songs and my son is going to do half of them so he can get into the mix.

Q. Can you give me a brief overview of the book?

A. Basically, *Numbers* is a story of a young boy who grew up in the projects hustling at an early age, as in running numbers, and then he started gambling dice, playing cards, and ended up in a hostile world of drug dealers. It's a story about his life, his trials and tribulations, and if he could ever get out of the street hustle or is he gone forever? So now he has to create an exit plan for himself. I wrote two screenplays too. I wrote *Cinderfella Dana Dane* as a screenplay and shopped that around. Regina King has been helping me to get that movie made. I've been producing a mini-series called *The Sty*, as in Bed Sty, and it's basically the Brooklyn version of the Wire—a six-part miniseries.

Q. What types of changes do you foresee in the future of Rap music?

A. Rap can be fused with any and everything. There is no limitation. It's been used with Rock, Hip-Hop Jazz, whatever. The sky is the limit. Whatever the next generation brings to it, that's where it's going to be going. I just hope to be able to watch it to see what they do with it because I know it's going to be incredible.

I was probably the first one to play a Rap record because there wasn't any Rap clubs, there were no radio stations, so the only venues you could really go is either to Harlem or give it to the street deejay, but I was the only commercial place where people would be able to hear it. I broke most of the records in the Fever. Kurtis Blow was the first one to give me a gold record 'cause I was probably the first one to play "Christmas Rhymes." When their [Sugarhill Gang] record went double-platinum, I was the first one to play "Rapper's Delight" in New York, so they gave me the record in being instrumental in helping them go double-platinum.
—Sal Abbatiello

The Fat Boys

Q. Who were the artists that influenced you guys when you were coming up in Hip-Hop?

A. Jimmy Spicer, you know he came out after Sugarhill, the Treacherous Three, Cold Crush 4, every cat that came up in that era wanted to rap like the Cold Crush 4, do the same kind of routines, you know, Mele Mel and the Furious 5, those guys really influenced us. The school that we came from, us, Run DMC, Whodini, L.L. Cool J, and the Beastie Boys pretty much set the standard because we were the first groups on MTV. We set the standard for a loose following in Hip-Hop, I would say, because gone were the days of the parks and studio bands inside the studio like the Funky Four did and taking songs and just rapping over them. Now, you have Larry Smith, who played a huge part in Run DMC's success and he came out with a whole new beat and, like you said, we came after the Furious 5 and the Cold Crush 4s and we were, like, the next school coming up.

Q. How old were you guys when "Reality" was released?

A. Ahh damn, I had just turned 17, Buff was going on 17, and Mark was 15. We were, like, youngsters. We were, like, wide-eyed and bushy-tailed. We didn't know anything of what was going on. All we wanted to do was buy a beat box and have people laugh at our music. We didn't care nothing about the signing of the contracts. We just wanted to be "hood famous" like they call it nowadays.

Q. How was the deal with record labels?

A. A lot of people were getting taken advantage of. A lot of people didn't know how many records they were selling. A lot of people were just satisfied hearing their names on the radio and getting a few thousand dollars in their pockets, not to put any of the cats down who came before us, but a lot of these cats are still living in the projects. They worked their way out of the projects, but are still living in the projects because the record companies didn't take care of them, just used them and went on to the next rapper.

Q. At one point when you guys released Fat Boys and changed your group name to the Fat Boys, you guys were really hot and Run-DMC was hot and you all were going neck to neck. Did you all view each other as competition?

A. Oh yeah, the thing with us and Run-DMC was so similar, not as far as the music part because they were more of a hardcore Rap group, they would curse on stage and we wouldn't curse, but as far as the jeans and the sneakers, just dressing ordinary, that was us. I think Whodini was more for the women. They were more of an R&B/Hip-Hop group. They were running around the hotels crazy bringing women to their rooms and we were just thinking along the lines of going to the room and have Buffy beat boxing, me and Mark against Run and DMC and we would just battle all night for four days at a time. We had a huge competition. They would come up to us sometimes and be like, "Y'all didn't sell 70,000 copies this week," and we would have to prove we did and they would come back and say, "Well, we sold 85,000 copies this week," so we were doing the back and forth thing. A lot of people misjudged us 'cause they thought all we did was Rap about this stuff, but they forgot we had to learn this from somewhere. We we're talking about the whole food thing because that's where the money was, but a lot of people mistook us from being like we were on records.

Q. What was it like being a part of Fresh Fest?

A. That was a lot of fun because you were with your peers, so it wasn't like you were with an R&B band. The thing that happened with Hip-Hop and the big bands of the 80s coming out the late 70s into the 80s was like, wow! We could just hook up turntables in ten minutes whereas with the big bands, like the SOS Band, Atlantic Star, and all those guys who were really popular at the time, but you had to take apart the whole set and put up another set for the next band, which would take up to a half an hour to an hour and with Hip-Hop, all you had to do was disconnect turntables and plug up your turntables and that would only take up to five to ten minutes. The thing with Fresh Fest is that nobody really knew where Hip-Hop was going. We knew it was getting hot and we would go to some of these places like North Carolina and South Carolina, but at the same time, a lot of radio stations wasn't really playing our music. They had to start playing it after that because the kids were requesting it. You couldn't stop it. It was just a moving force you couldn't stop. By the time we got to some of these cities, the hotels would be, like, five to ten thousand people in front of the hotels alone just waiting for us to pull up. It was like a huge phenomenon. It was like no one was prepared for it. The Fresh Fest was just fun. It was like a 24 hour thing where nobody really got no sleep. We were like freaking mad men.

Q. Did anything escalate to a battle between Buffy and Dougie Fresh?

A. Oh yeah, they were competitive. We were in Dallas at a show and it was 20,000 strong was out there and Dougie Fresh was hot with the show, "La Di Da Di" and they were going on before us and he and Buff were going back and forth just talking crap to one another, "You can't mess with me," "I sold this many records. How many did you sell?" "We just turned gold," "Oh, we were gold, like, a year ago." Buff went out there and just ripped it that night. It was the best I had ever seen him do it because he was just so amped that night from Doug talking so much junk. He tore the house down. Buff was the only one, to me, that really sounded like a drum because he had the bass down pat. He didn't do any animated stuff like a computer sound with his mouth. He just wanted to do the beat, bass, and snare.

Q. What is your greatest moment in Hip-Hop?

A. In 1988, we were invited to the Grammys coming on the heels of the success from the *Crushin'* album and we sat in the front row and Michael Jackson performed "Man in the Mirror" and at the end of the show, somebody came and invited us on the stage for the grand finale with the other acts that performed that night. Michael Jackson just turned to us and shook our hand and he said how much he admired us. He told us how hard we worked and he said, "When I turn on my TV, you guys are everywhere!" We were on cloud nine then. We were driving home saying, "Michael Jackson just gave us props!"

The Dedication

18 lines of sunlight
Shining in between each window blind
Not sure if it's time or being in your arms
That left last night's darkness behind
It's like walking in the rain for days
To see nothing but the beauty of a rainbow
I found you standing at the end of it
And never will gold have the same glow
Never knew how precious a second could be
Until the first second we were apart
I would fight and push back the hands of time
So that second wouldn't have to start
All it takes is just one smile
To feel blessed to have a dream come true

Made me realize God has the world in his hands
The way I have mine when I'm holding you
You're as beautiful as pink rose petals
Floating in a lake on top of the water
And you must be an angel from heaven
Or my time on earth was much shorter
And when there's 18 lines of darkness
Shadowed in between each window blind
All I have to do is hold you
And once again the sun has shined

Hip Hop Hooray

Hip Hop History in Photos

Dr. Dre and Jay-Z

Hip Hop Hooray

LL Cool J

Hip Hop History in Photos

Kokane

Grandmaster Flash and the Furious 5

Hip Hop Hooray

Rock Master Scott & The Dynamic Three

The Fat Boys

Big Daddy Kane

Dana Dane

Hip Hop Hooray

Doug E. Fresh, Charlie Prince, and KRS One

Kid N Play

Kool Rock Biopic

Biz Markie

Will Smith

Hip Hop History in Photos

Queen Latifah

Hip Hop Hooray

MC Lyte

Snoop Dogg

Diddy

Hip Hop History in Photos

Lost Boyz

Queen Pen

MC Hammer

Kurtis Blow

Hip Hop History in Photos

DMX

Ice Cube

Hip Hop Hooray

Michael Jackson and Quincy Jones

Hip Hop History in Photos

Wu Tang Clan

Soul Sonic Force

Hip Hop Hooray

Sean XLG

Eight

1990 Flashback

1990 is the year that Hip-Hop celebrated its fifteenth anniversary with *Rapmania: The Roots of Rap*. *Rapmania* was a televised live event with explosive performances from two stages, The Palace in Los Angeles and The Apollo Theater in New York. The event was put together and promoted by Hip-Hop pioneer Van Silk and co-hosted by Fab 5 Freddy of *Yo! MTV Raps* along with actress/choreographer Debbie Allen. The event included interviews with such legends as Grandmaster Flash and Afrika Bambaataa and became a memorable event with over two hours of hardcore performances of some of the biggest stars in Rap music.

The show opened with a dazzling introduction by Grandmaster Melle Mel, the first of many stars to grace the stage, to include Young M.C., Prince Whipper Whip, Biz Markie, Everlast, and Whodini performing their mega hit "Friends." Kurtis Blow performed a medley of his hits while Ice-T, Tone Loc, Special K, Big Daddy Kane, Slick Rick, and Nefertiti were just a few of the many stars who hit the stage. From Eric B. and Rakim, L.L. Cool J, and Grandmaster Caz, to 3rd Base, the show was an equal balance of old-school and new-school artists. The *USA Today* featured a full-length article on *Rapmania* with colorful photographs of Run-DMC and Kool Moe Dee performing during the event. It goes without saying that *Rapmania* turned out enormously successful.

The 2 Live Crew released the LP *Banned In the U.S.A.*, a title reflecting the controversy they faced regarding their recent albums; Ice Cube released the LP *Amerikkka's Most Wanted* and was certified platinum; Everlast, an Ice T. protégé, dropped "Forever Everlasting;" King Tee made noise with the hot cut "Played Like A Piano;" and Big Daddy Kane came out with the LP, *Taste of Chocolate* and scored with the up-beat single, "It's Hard Being The Kane."

The Boo Yaa Tribe hit the underground scene and made noise on the West Coast while Boogie Down Productions dropped the album *Edutainment*, featuring the top ten R&B/Hip-Hop single, "Love's Gonna Getcha';" An unfortunate accident took place at a Heavy D concert and band member Trouble T-Roy was fatally injured; D-Nice made noise with the cut, "Call Me D-Nice;" EPMD hit us with "Business As Usual;" Brand Nubian came out with the LP *One For All*; and Will Smith, otherwise known as The Fresh Prince, starred in the then-new NBC sitcom *The Fresh Prince of Bel Air*. The theme song started out, "In West Philadelphia born and raised, on the playgrounds is where I spent most of my days…"

Public Enemy released the highly anticipated LP *Fear of a Black Planet*; GZA signed to Cold Chillin' Records and put out *Words From the Genius;* Ice Cube returned with back-to-back platinum albums with the release of *Kill At Will*, featuring the hit singles, "Dead Homies" and "Jackin' For Beats;" L.L. Cool J dropped the album *Momma Said Knock You Out* with the hit singles "Boomin' System" and "Around The Way Girl," including the title cut, "Momma Said Knock You Out," which reached double-platinum status.

Kool G. Rap and D.J. Polo dropped the LP *Wanted: Dead or Alive* and smoked with the single, "Streets of New York;" Run-DMC returned with the new album *Back From Hell* and rode the charts with the cut, "Pause;" Salt 'N Pepa dropped the platinum joint *Black's Magic* featuring the smash hits, "Expression" and "Let's Talk About Sex;" Too Short hit the scene with Short Dog's *In The House*, a platinum

LP; and Young M.C. walked away with the Grammy Award for Best Rap Performance for "Bust A Move."

Kid 'N Play released the LP *Fun House* and starred in the hit film *House Party* with comedian Martin Lawrence and R&B group Full Force; The X-Clan scored with the release "To The East;" Blackwards and dance band C&C Music Factory burned the charts with the joint, "Gonna Make You Sweat (Everybody Dance Now)," peaking at #1 on Billboard's Hot 100 Singles chart; Kwame came out with, "A Day In the Life;" Sir Mix-A-Lot scored big with the comical cut, "My Hooptie'" and I, Sean XLG, became the first rapper to win a national music competition on the syndicated radio show *Radioscope*.

M.C. Hammer followed up his triple-platinum debut LP with "Please Hammer Don't Hurt 'Em." This LP would forever change the face of Rap music. Up to this point, Rap had big stars and popular crossover artists, but M.C. Hammer became Hip Hop's first mega-star. The album rode the heat from the multi-platinum single, "U Can't Touch This." *Please Hammer Don't Hurt 'Em* became the first Rap album to surpass platinum status and reach the Diamond mark, exceeding 10 million sales.

Please Hammer Don't Hurt 'Em hit #1 on Billboard's Top 200 Albums chart and remained there for an unprecedented 21 weeks. It was now the biggest selling Rap album of all time with mega hit singles, "Have You Seen Her," "Pray," and "Dancin' Machine." Hammer became the Michael Jackson of Hip-Hop as a result of his success and popularity. Mostly known for his live stage performances and dance routines, Hammer transcended Rap like no other artist.

The phrase "Hammer Time" became popular slang on the streets. M.C. Hammer action figures hit toy stores all over the country and a cartoon series called *Hammer Time* hit the television airwaves. However, due to his overwhelming success and clean-cut image, Hammer soon became the target of criticism in the Hip-Hop community. A number of his counterparts, from both East and West coasts, began a campaign to oust Hammer from his throne as the king of Hip-Hop. Hammer was now the victim of an onslaught dis attack.

Dana Dane dropped the LP *Dana Dane Forever*; Digital Underground made noise with *Sex Packets* featuring the platinum single, "The Humpty Dance;" Father M.C., a protégé of Sean Puffy Combs, scored a hit with "I'll Do 4 U," a smooth cut with an R&B feel.

Following the mainstream success of Hammer, Vanilla Ice released *To The Extreme* featuring the mega hit, "Ice Ice Baby." The LP also reached Diamond status. Vanilla Ice, as result of reaching Hammer's plateau in terms of success, also bore the blunt of criticism from other artists.

In the spirit of the Stop The Violence Movement and the hit single, "Self Destruction," activist Michael Concepcion formed The West Coast All-Stars—a collaboration of artists to include Above The Law, Digital Underground, Dr. Dre, Eazy E., M.C. Hammer, Tone Loc, and R&B sensation Michel'le, among others, to record the anti-gang message, "We're All In The Same Gang." Ice T rhymed:

> What if we could take our enemies and feed 'em poison
> Under-educate their girls and boys and
> Twist 'em up and make 'em kill each other
> Better yet, make 'em kill for a color

The single was popular and the project helped to make an impact in combating the rash of gang violence in the L.A. area. In addition to Ice T's participation in the anti-gang movement, he, along with Big Daddy Kane, Grandmaster Melle Mel, and Kool Moe Dee received the Grammy Award for Best Rap Performance By A Duo Or Group for the *Back On The Block* project.

"My greatest moments in Hip-Hop are when I first heard "Rockin' It" on the radio during the Frankie Crocker show; being at the Audubon and seeing Grandmaster Flash doing the beat box live; the very first time I was at Harlem World and I saw the legendary Cold Crush Brothers; and when Kool Moe Dee battled Busy Bee—that was classic."
—Mighty Mike C from the Fearless 4

Hip Hop Hooray

Nine

Bring Da Noise

Bling Into Fashion

The untimely shooting deaths of Rap stars Tupac Shakur and The Notorious B.I.G. sent a shock wave throughout the Hip-Hop community. As a result, a number of rappers responded in a very unusual manner with bulletproof attire. Hip-Hop celebrities from Diddy and Ice-T to Queen Latifah paid in excess of $15,000.00 for death-resistant clothing that included mink coats, Kevlar-coated baseball caps and shot-retardant raincoats. Along with bulletproof pants, jackets, and specially-made jock straps, Hip-Hop gave a new meaning to the word "fashion."

The X Factor

The summer of 1990 marked the date when I, Sean XLG, became the first Rap artist to win a national music competition. The contest took place on Lee Bailey's syndicated program *Radioscope*, a show where contestants' songs were played and the listening audience called in their votes to choose the winner. In short, *Radioscope* was the radio equivalent of what American Idol is today. The song that I entered into the contest was called "The Johnsons," a comical Rap about a father and son dialog. The song won three consecutive times and never lost during the competition.

Rap-A-Lot

Amid controversy regarding music censorship, political pressure, a distribution deal gone bad, and virtually no airplay on the radio, the Geto Boys released the LP *We Can't Be Stopped* and earned platinum status. It was 1999 and the album's lead single was the hit song "Mind Playin' Tricks On Me." The popularity of the song overshadowed the sobering album cover showing, in graphic detail, group member Bushwick Bill on a hospital stretcher after losing an eye in a shooting accident. The controversial cover undoubtedly created a buzz that boosted album sales and the group took advantage of the publicity.

Party UP

In January 1999, none other than DMX, the first artist in history to top the charts twice in a single calendar year, knocked Country music sensation Garth Brooks off of Billboard's top album spot. DMX is also the first artist to debut at number 1 on the billboard Pop charts with his first five albums:

- *It's Dark and Hell is Hot*
- *Flesh of My Flesh, Blood of My Blood*
- *And Then There Was X*
- *The Great Depression*
- *Grand Champ*
- His 6th album, *Year of the Dog...Again* barely missed the top spot and came in at number two.

Doggy Style

Dr. Dre first introduced Snoop Dog to the world with his classic album *The Chronic*. The album was a multi-platinum masterpiece and the two artists collaborated on the mega-hits "Nuthin' But a G Thang," "Dre Day," and "Let Me Ride." The success of the album created much-anticipated hype surrounding Snoop and by 1993, he released his LP *Doggy Style* and it entered the charts at number 1, the first time ever for a debut album.

Slim Shady

Eminem is one of the most successful Rap artists in the history of Hip-Hop. His 1999 debut album *Slim Shady* made a lot of noise and featured the hit single "My Name Is" and was certified multi-platinum. By the summer of 2000, Eminem released the *Marshall Mathers* LP, selling close to 2 million copies in its first week of release, earning a spot in the Guinness Book of World Records as the fastest selling Rap album of all time. The album reached the number 1 spot on five different music charts and sold over 22 million copies around the world.

Shake Ya Ass

The hit-making wonders known as the Neptunes emerged on the Hip-Hop scene in 1999 from out of Virginia Beach. They produced such hits as "Got My Money" by Old Dirty Bastard and "Shake Ya Ass" by Mystikal. The dynamic duo crossed over to the Pop charts in 2001 and scored hits for Usher and Britney Spears, ultimately becoming the most sought-after producers in the music industry. They have also produced hits for Jay-Z, Busta Rhymes, and Snoop Dog.

Speakerboxxx

Andre 3000 and Big Boi are the hit-making duo better known as Outkast. Exploding on the scene in 1994 with *Player's Ball*, Outkast reached number 1 on the Rap charts. The crew helped to put ATL and the Dirty South in the forefront of Hip-Hop. Their first album *Southernplayalisticadillacmuzik* was a huge success that surpassed platinum status. A number of mega-hits followed like "Ms. Jackson," "B.O.B.," and "Hey Ya." They ventured into making movies starring in *Idlewild, Four Brothers,* and *ATL* and are one of a few Rap acts to reach Diamond status with their hit LP *Speakerboxxx/The Love Below*.

Supa Dupa Fly

Missy Elliot debuted in 1997 with the LP *Supa Dupa Fly* featuring the hit song "The Rain." Shortly afterwards, "The Rain" was followed by the 1999 chart toppers, "She's A Bitch" and "Hot Boyz."

Produced by the one and only Timbaland, Missy's classics include "Work It" and "Get Ur Freak On," delivered with her signature flare and unorthodox, creative flow. Recording success lead to Missy's mainstream appeal and, subsequently, advertising ventures for the soft drink Sprite, Gap clothing line, and, ultimately, making Missy a Hip-Hop superstar in the game.

The Miseducation Of Lauryn Hill

Lauryn Hill, one third of the Hip-Hop powerhouse The Fugees, released a solo LP in 1998 titled *The Miseducation Of Lauryn Hill*. The multi-talented singer, producer and songwriter contributed to 90% of the songs on the album that included such hits as "Doo Wop (That Thing)," and "Every Ghetto, Every City," to name a few. The album fused Hip-Hop, Reggae, and old school R&B to became an instant classic. Hill received 11 nominations at the 1999 Grammy Awards, winning five—the most ever won by a woman.

California Love

2Pac, the one-time member and dancer for the Rap group Digital Underground, rocked the world of Hip-Hop with his 1991 debut LP *2Pacalypse Now*, spawning the hit single "Brenda's Got A Baby" and was certified gold. The success of the album ran parallel with his growing popularity from acting after starring in the film "Juice." 2Pac's next album *Strictly for My N.I.G.G.A.Z.* went platinum and released the hits "Keep Ya' Head Up" and "I Get Around." By the time his third LP, *Me Against the World* dropped, 2Pac was serving a 4-year prison sentence for sexual assault. Nevertheless, the album entered the charts at number 1, the first time in history for an artist incarcerated.

Down 4 U

None other than Ja Rule spearheaded the rise of the record label Murder Inc. The Irv Gotti-produced Rap star single-handidly put the label on the map while cranking out hits like "Holla, Holla" and duet smashes like "Between Me and You," and "Put It On Me." Not only did Ja Rule's success make him one of the premier Rap artists of the 2000's, but also it launched the career of R&B sensation Ashanti.

Guinness World Record

Speed Rap was invented in 1978 by the legendary Kool Mo Dee. The 1980 Hip-Hop classic "The New Rap Language" by Kool Mo Dee's group The Treacherous Three showcased Speed Rap at its finest. By 1992, Twista, a Chicago-based emcee, reinvented the Speed Rap by making it even faster. So fast, in fact, he was recognized by the Guinness Book Of World Records for the fastest Rap flow in the world.

Things That Make You Go Hmmm?

January 2, 1989 is the date when the Arsenio Hall Show first aired on national television. The popular comedian-actor hosted the first late night talk show that catered to an urban audience. Among many of his guests were President Bill Clinton, Michael Jordan, Madonna, and Minister Farrakhan, along with numerous Rap acts featured as musical guests. After five seasons on the air, the show ended on May 27, 1994. As a grand finale on the final episode, an all-star lineup of rappers hit the stage for one last time. KRS-One, Wu Tang Clan, M.C. Lyte, Yo-Yo, Das Efx, CL Smooth, A Tribe Called Quest, Treach, Mad Lion and Fu-Schnickens performed freestyle to pay tribute to Arsenio Hall and the performance was absolutely bananas!

The Source

In November of 1993, *The Source* magazine dedicated its 50th issue to Hip-Hop history. The cover featured the founding fathers of the movement: Grandmaster Flash, Afrika Bambaataa, and Kool DJ Herc. The pioneering DJs told the story of the origins of Hip-Hop from deejaying and rapping to break-dancing and graffiti. Additionally, the magazine covers the history of Hip-Hop from top to bottom with a spread of old school fliers, articles on artists, and trivia that tested your knowledge of Hip-Hop!

Hip-Hop Holiday

Memorial Day in 1991 is noted as the Hip-Hop Holiday at the Apollo Theater in Harlem. The show had remarkable performances by Nikki D, Leaders of the New School, Shelly Thunder, Brand Nubians, Run-DMC, and Reggae standout Shabba Ranks headlined. Two shows were scheduled and both concerts played to sold out crowds. The event was co-hosted by turntable wizard Kid Capri.

The Chronic

The Chronic, released in 1992 by master producer Dr. Dre, is noted as one of the greatest Rap albums of all time. The debut solo album from the former NWA member reached the number three spot on the Billboard 200 and launched Dr. Dre into the spotlight as a musical genius. The album rode the charts on the strength of hit singles "Nuthin' But A 'G' Thang," "Dre Day," and "Let Me Ride," featuring collaborations with and the debut of Snoop Dog. The album sold over three million copies and was certified as triple-platinum. *The Chronic* currently ranks #137 on Rolling Stone's list of the 500 Greatest Albums of All time.

Hall of Fame Hits

"FAT BOYS"—FAT BOYS

"HOT IN HERRE"—NELLY

"WHAT A MAN"—SALT 'N PEPA

"SEEN A MAN DIE"—SCARFACE

"HIP HOP HOORAY"—NAUGHTY BY NATURE

"I CAN'T LIVE WITHOUT MY RADIO"—LL COOL J

"O.P.P."—NAUGHTY BY NATURE

"I KNOW YOU GOT SOUL"—ERIC B & RAKIM

"MY MIND'S PLAYIN TRICKS ON ME"—GETO BOYS

"FIVE MINUTES OF FUNK"—WHODINI

"JUST A FRIEND"—BIZ MARKIE

"ROCKIT"—HERBIE HANCOCK FEATURING GRANDMIXER DST

"LOLLI POP"—LIL WAYNE

"6 IN THE MORNING"—ICE T

Hip Hop Hooray

Ten

Pump Up The Bass

Interview with Arrested Development

Q. Who were the artists that influenced you when you first came up in music?

A. Speech: There's so many. Jackson 5, KISS, Spinners, QUEEN, O-Jay's, Marvin Gaye, Chicago, Stevie Wonder, and Prince, to name just a few. Then, of course, since The Sugarhill gang came out, there's been a slew of others!

A. Eshe: Wow! I've been influenced by so many artists in the realm of performing arts. My mom is a great influence on me, Tina Turner, Donnie Hathaway, RUN DMC, Al Green, Salt 'N Pepa, Alvin Ailey (Dance Company), Prince, Queen Latifah, Will Smith, BDP, Duran Duran, Devo, etc. The list just keeps going and going!

Q. In the early 90s, "Gangsta Rap" was becoming the most dominant form of Hip-Hop. How were you able to maintain your creative expressions in songs like "Tennessee" and "People Everyday" without conforming to the industry standards?

A. Speech: That was part of the point of our group! To NOT conform to the industry's standards and create a new pathway for artists to go down. We tried Gangster Rap when we first got together; it felt unnatural. What ultimately came out was the most honest form of expression and the world confirmed that it was the right way to go.

A. Eshe: In the early 90s, our style was very different from what was being played on the radio, in clubs, etc. We were just young people—newcomers to the game—doing what came naturally—being ourselves. We always strive to uplift people through our music, so we weren't willing to compromise our integrity. The creative expressions for songs like "Tennessee" & "People Everyday" came from personal experiences that happened in Speech's life. The loss of his grandmother & brother within the same week birthed Hip-Hop anthems.

Q. Your music has a positive, afro-centric vibe to it. Do you feel a certain responsibility to your fans and to Hip-Hop in general to create good, soulful music that you can party and dance to or just listen to?

A. Speech: We want to do both—create songs you can dance to and be ourselves in what we write about. My parents were both activists. We sat around the breakfast table talking about issues within the Black community as I was a kid. They also were both journalists. My mom still owns the largest Black newspaper in the state of Wisconsin (The Milwaukee Community Journal). So, talking about things that can offer solutions is still burning in my heart! I feel the pain of my people as you see fatherless homes, cycles of poverty that affect generations of families and children. Years of oppression and abuse have wreaked havoc not only on the African-American culture, but because of Hip-hop, that same brainwashing and low self-esteem has been broadcasted throughout the entire globe reaching all races! The Bible says the sins of the fathers will be passed down to future generations for three to four generations! That is what's happening now! Slavery was a grave sin and now the effects of slavery are becoming seen, even through White kids, who are the biggest patrons of Hip-Hop music.

A. Eshe: We create our music from our heart & soul and we have so much fun doing it. We always try to paint a vivid picture to bring people into our world, our lives, our experience. I would say that Arrested Development definitely feels a certain responsibility to our fans to stay creative, go against the grain, present thought-provoking issues, and produce quality music. Arrested Development is an experience; a movement! We want everyone to enjoy our music from a little baby to an elder. We have to have everyone out of their seats dancing, singing, and feeling free.

Q. If you weren't doing music, what profession or activities do you think you would be involved in?

A. Speech: I love teaching. I think I'd do that if I weren't a musician.

A. Eshe: If I weren't doing music, I would probably be a dancer in the world renowned dance company Alvin Ailey, a teacher, or working it out as a lawyer. It's funny because when I'm not touring, I teach young people, so I guess you can say I'm living my dream. To this day, to dance with Alvin Ailey is still a dream of mine and that would change my world forever.

Q. What do you feel are the positives and negatives of Rap music today, if any?

A. Speech: It has now made an impact on the whole world! Today's Hip-Hop is accepted as Pop music and the trends & clothing as well. The culture that comes within the music is capitalized on by present artists, which, in the past, was not an option. In some ways, this is positive. It allows some people to get rich, etc. BUT, I don't think it's as positive as many would say. I think there's a lot of SPIN going on with all the positivity of today's Hip-Hop artists. For instance, sure, a "gangsta" rapper may give $300,000 to inner-city youth through their foundation. When you look at the numbers, it's impressive, but if you compare the damage to the healing, there's actually NO comparison.

Their records spread to hundreds of millions of people around the globe ignorance, degradation towards women, horrible and damaging stereotypes about Blacks, and women that started centuries ago during slavery, misogyny, sexual irresponsibility, extreme materialism, violence, and sometimes, even Satanism. I can't tell you how many people around the planet think that ALL Blacks from America are riding around in Hummers, sporting gold chains and teeth with multiple women hanging on 'em.

A. Eshe: Well, the positive is that lots of people are eating and you have artist who are CEOs now. Artists are creating platforms, cross-promoting in all areas of entertainment, creating opportunities for other artists, etc. People are changing their realities and that's beautiful. On the flip side of that, as others are progressing, others are hurting. There is no balance on radio. It's too much of this and not enough of that. Its unfortunate 'cause back in the day, you had so much to choose from and it all had its place. Now, everything sounds, looks, and feels the same. There are some many great artists out here that's presenting something different from what we hear on main stream radio, however, you never hear about them because they're not given the opportunity. I think if we focus on making great, timeless, life-changing, classic music, as a whole, music would be in a better place than it is today.

Q. Can you tell us something about the new recording project you're working on and what we can look forward to from Arrested Development?

A. Speech: WE'RE EXCITED about *STRONG,* our newest project! It's really hot! It's filled with raw emotion, great beats, and tight lyrics. It's already hit the top 10 in Japan and Jakarta (Indonesia). We are presently touring this album around the world from London to Australia. It's out now at: www.ArrestedDevelopmentMusic.com

A. Eshe: Yes! Our new album is called *STRONG* and we're very excited about it! We're still staying true to what Arrested Development has always been about. This album has so many influences from classic Hip-Hop, Funk, Rock, World Music. It's thought-provoking, fun, conscious, family-oriented, soulful, and just a feel-good record. We call our music LIFE MUSIC and that's truly what it is!

Q. What is your greatest moment in Hip-Hop?

A. Speech: I've had too many to name one, but one of 'em was the summer of '89 when Public Enemy was the hottest group out in Rap. I was so inspired by what Hip-Hop was doing and where it was going! Some really great music came out during the late eighties and early nineties (the Golden Era).

A. Eshe: My greatest moments in Hip-Hop had to be the Tom Joyner Cruise 2010. Mr. Joyner dedicated a night to Hip-Hop and the show was called *Back to Black*. The show was filled with Hip-Hop legends: Biz Markie, Common, Doug E. Fresh, Arrested Development, EPMD, Monie Love, Roxanne Shante', The Fat Boys, Naughty By Nature, DJ Kool, DJ Scratch. Minister Farrakhan came out and gave everyone on the stage a charge to be responsible with our lyrics and he spoke on how we have so much POWER to change the world. Minister Farrakhan ended his speech by giving all of us love and a special shout out to ARRESTED DEVELOPMENT. WOW! What a moment! I'll never forget that as long as I live!

Obra Maestra

The pen and the paper
Together gave birth
To the greatest creation
Since the making of earth
When I grab the mic
I not only rock well
But I blow up the spot
Like a Molotov cocktail
Cause lyrics are lethal
And can do more harm
Than a needle with a
Belt tied around your arm
A yo, I pen poetry
'Til psychologists suppose
That I suffer from chronic
Rhythmic neurosis
As I gave the microphone
Electrical spasms
And gave the crowd
A hard sweating orgasm
More than a lyrical lord
I'm the presence
Of a greater creator
Exalted by the essence
So when I put the microphone
Down smoke lingers
If you tried sign language
My rhymes would break fingers
And once they enshrine
Every line they'll design
My mic have it bronzed
And encased in Palestine

You can't be from Florida and not know Uncle Luke, 2 Live Crew, and the 69 Boys with the Tootsie Roll. We rolled it up for years. In this particular market, we like to dance like popping and locking and those particular artists, they influenced those types of dance moves. You know JZ Money and Trick Daddy, they opened the doors for a lot of artists in Florida coming out right now.

—Kaneri Diamond

Interview with Kokane "The Hook Master"

Q. Can you tell me about EWA?

A. EWA stands for East coast, West coast Alliance and, basically, it's a project to bring both coasts together. The styles of both coast are very much alike. The dress code, the music, and the East coast, that's the Mecca of Hip-Hop. So to bring the two together is what we're trying to do. This is not to exclude the South because they're doing their thing. We just want to be a part of it so that we can all work together. I'm pretty much in touch with everybody; Dr. Dre, Too Short, DJ Quick, Above the Law, Kurupt, and others out West and on the East coast, we've been in touch with Prince Paul, Jada, Busta Rhymes, Redman and Method Man, Puffy; I'm reaching out to everybody. Also, we want to modify positivity between East coast and West coast because, if you look way back around 16, 17 years ago, you had the "Self Destruction" cause, and then, on the flip side, on the West coast we had "We're All In The Same Gang" with Dr. Dre and all the West coast artists, so it's really a unification thru the music, style, culture. To break down that barrier to the South, and we're bridging gaps, that's what it's all about. So it's definitely a project that's going to be huge in terms of Hip-Hop and it should be completed sometime in 2009. It's going to be a mass explosion.

Q. What are your greatest moments in Hip-Hop?

A. Two of the greatest shows I ever did had to be a part of a NWA concert. I've seen a whole lot of concerts, been on tour and everything, and there was nobody that made an impact like NWA. When they came out and said, "Fuck the Police!" you talk about hype?! One of the greatest things in Hip-Hop, at a time when I first started, was seeing my twin boys born because NWA and Easy-E and them drove up to the hospital. Me and my wife, seeing our kids born, and we put them in the video. That was my greatest time right there. And third is being on stage at the 2004 ESPY Awards with Parliament. It was a dream come true because George was sick in the Netherlands somewhere, so they asked me to fill in for George and people were like, "You sound like George Clinton!"

Q. Can you tell me about your reality television show?

A. This reality show is kind of different from any other reality show. It's showing different elements and one of the elements its showing is the side of Hip-Hop fatherhood because, as you know, I'm a married man with 20 years and I got 8 kids by one woman, so it's showing the highs and lows, especially from the standpoint of a person being in the music industry for a long time and also shows interacting with these great people—who is this person behind the most featured artist in the world? This man named Jerry Long/Kokane? It shows interaction with various artists from Cameo to Dr. Dre and anybody and the moral message of the show is even though we're in the business and its so materialistic and high-fashion about selling records, its one thing that stands clear is showing the positive side about family inside the house and me and my family being out on the town, so, basically, the best thing you can have in the music industry is family to not only sustain you, but ground you and show how the family goes out to church and it's more of reality as opposed to other shows that's more scripted. Me and Earnest wanted to show the real side. We didn't want to concentrate on so much violence to sell the show. We wanted to show the impact of a person who's been in the music industry and the extension of success of being on everybody's hooks. It's called *The Legendary Mr. Kane Show* and its every bit up to the name.

Hall of Fame Hits

"BUST A MOVE"—YOUNG MC

"IT'S HARD OUT HERE FOR A PIMP"—THREE 6 MAFIA

"A FLY GIRL"—THE BOOGIE BOYS

"FUNKY COLD MEDINA"—TONE LOC

"TENNESSEE"—ARRESTED DEVELOPMENT

"LOOKING FOR THE PERFECT BEAT"—AFRIKA BAMBAATAA & THE SOUL SONIC FORCE

"RUMP SHAKER"—WRECKS-N-EFFECT

"ME SO HORNY"—2 LIVE CREW

"FIGHT THE POWER"—PUBLIC ENEMY

"WHITE LINES"—MELLE MEL

"8TH WONDER"—SUGARHILL GANG

"LA DI DA DI"—DOUG E FRESH & THE GET FRESH CREW

"SUCKER MCs"—RUN-DMC

"NO TIME FOR FAKE"—LIL' KIM

Hip Hop Hooray

Eleven

The Roof Is On Fire

Empire State Of Mind

"In New York, concrete jungle where dreams are made...."

Jay-Z has a plethora of great moments in Hip-Hop, including receiving GQ's International Man of the Year award. What may stand out to most is his 2008 contract with concert promoter Live Nation for $150 million, one of the highest-paid contracts ever awarded to a musical artist. Roc Nation, the name of the partnership between Live Nation and Jay-Z, includes financing for Jay-Z's entertainment ventures from a record label and concerts to business investments. The deal is reportedly more than the contracts with U2 and Madonna and includes an upfront payment of $25 million as well as advances for tours and $10 million per album for a minimum of three albums during a ten-year term.

Yo! MTV Raps

In 2007, MTV honored *Yo! MTV Raps* as its most influential music series of all time. The show, created by late filmmaker Ted Demme and Peter Doughtery, was MTV's first predominately Black music series. Debuting in August 1988 to a national audience, the video show helped Rap music become a worldwide phenomenon. Hosted by legendary graffiti artist Fab Five Freddy, the show brought artists from De La Soul and Too Short to Big Daddy Kane and MC Lyte to mainstream status. Dr. Dre and Ed Lover later joined Fab Five Freddy as hosts of a weekly spinoff of the groundbreaking music program. The emergence of *Yo! MTV Raps* was a significant moment in Hip-Hop, bringing dozens of artists and their music into the spotlight and it served as one, if not the biggest, component in the advancement of Hip-Hop culture.

Recognize!

On February 8, 2008, the Smithsonian's National Portrait Gallery in Washington, DC opened the exhibition titled *RECOGNIZE! Hip Hop and Contemporary Portraiture*. The National Portrait Gallery of the Smithsonian Institution featured graffiti murals and Hip-Hop artists such as Big Daddy Kane, Notorious B.I.G., Tupac, L.L. Cool J, and Grandmaster Flash and the Furious Five. In addition, a photography exhibit by David Scheinbaum was on display with Black and white photos of Common, Talib Kwali, Prince Paul, Nas, and Jurassic 5 MCs, among others. This was further proof that a picture is worth 1,000 words!

Hip Hop 4 HIV

The *Hip Hop 4 HIV: Know Your Status* concert kicked off at the Reliant Stadium in Houston, TX and drew a record number of teenagers and young adults. An estimated 7,500 people showed up in what was reported as the largest single HIV testing event in US history! The performers, Bun B, Lil' Wayne, Birdman, David Banner, and UGK, were featured at the event that was sponsored by the Tex Stars Foundation, a non-profit organization that assists inner-city communities. While the reputations of some of the artists performing may border on questionable in the eyes of mainstream America, their participation in such a worthy event underscored the positive contribution of their music and focus.

It Takes A Nation of Millions

The New York Hilton Hotel hosted the first conference, *Hip-Hop Summit: Taking Back Responsibility*, a two day event organized by Hip-Hop mogul Russell Simmons. The conference included such

Hip-Hop notables as Sean "Diddy" Combs, Chuck D, Queen Latifah, and Fat Joe. Grandmaster Flash and Naughty By Nature were also in attendance. Nation of Islam leader Minister Louis Farrakhan provided the keynote address. The conference presented ways of strengthening the social, political, and economical impact Rap music has on society at large. This is just one of the many social causes Russell Simmons championed. The importance of such work and effort is why the summits consistently add to the shine of one of Hip-Hop's true giants.

The Green Initiative

At a New York City press conference, Hip-Hop mogul Russell Simmons announced the launching of a new jewelry line, the Green Initiative. Manufactured and designed by the Simmons Jewelry Company, 25% of proceeds from sales would go towards the new Diamond Empowerment Fund, which will support institutions like schools and colleges in South Africa and Botswana, in particular, and help boost economic development on the African continent. The Initiative is reflective of the social awareness and responsibility that Russell Simmons embraces and serves as a shining example for others to utilize their positions of influence and power in meaningful ways. Africa, what better place to start?!

It's Like That

Pioneering Rap group Run-DMC celebrated their induction into Hollywood's RockWalk in 2006. Run-DMC, whose hits include, "Sucker M.C.'s," "My Adidas," and the crossover smash, "Walk This Way," became the first Rap act to imprint their hands on Hollywood's prestigious RockWalk. Credited as the first Rap act to bring the art form into Pop culture, Run-DMC paved the way for the mainstream appeal Rap music has today. For more than a decade, the trio from Hollis, Queens advanced the musical sounds and polished the stylish image of the genre. They single-handedly redefined Hip-Hop and bridged the art form from the old school's "yes-yes y'all" heydays to the next generation's funky fresh appeal. Run-DMC's induction was a perfect befitting for the Kings of Rock!

Jus Us 4 Jackie

In 2003, hit Rap artist Nelly, along with his late sister, Jackie Donahue, formed Jus Us 4 Jackie, a nationwide bone marrow donor drive recruitment campaign conducted through Nelly's non-profit 4 Sho' 4 Kids Foundation. The donor drive in St. Louis made history as the most successful African-American bone marrow registry drive, attracting more than 1,200 people. As a result of the Foundation's work, Nelly was presented with the Napoleon Harris Foundation Philanthropy Award during a celebrity gala and fundraiser at the Chicago Marriott Hotel.

The Half Mill Grill

Cash Money Records CEO, the Birdman, made the list with the biggest bling of all time. The Birdman replaced a $250,000 set of platinum with white gold-plated and diamond encrusted crowns with a $500,000 set of 18 karat white gold and platinum crowns set with ascher-cut diamonds. The 17 crowns are supported by his natural teeth and are insured for $700,000. After a six-hour procedure for the cosmetic dentistry, the Birdman can flash a million dollar smile.

H2 Oh Yeah!

Hip-hop mega star Jay-Z is just as fluid with rhymes as he is with aqua. Jay-Z met with United Nations Secretary General Kofi Annan and discussed the millions of people currently living without clean drinking water and proper sanitation. In an effort to give back, Jay-Z created the *Diary of Jay-Z: Water for Life* to bring attention to the water crisis around the world. In addition, Jay-Z plans to build 1,000 "play pumps" in Africa to supply water for people in need. Jay-Z is not only a musical genius capable of spitting flows and selling platinum albums, but his commitment to such worthy causes is one of the many reasons why he garners the respect that he has on and off the stage!

Holy Hip Hop

For years, spiritual messages have been incorporated into Rap music. Artists from Rakim and Big Daddy Kane, KRS-One, M.C. Hammer and the Poor Righteous Teachers, among others, have enlightened fans with various inspirational teachings from the Five-Percent Nation to Christianity and Islam. However, Holy Hip-Hop has taken the message to a higher level. Rap pioneer Kurtis Blow is the founder of a contemporary church in Harlem that incorporates Hip-Hop in its ministry.

Kurtis Blow, widely known for the classic hits, "Christmas Rappin'" and "The Breaks," brings across the church's message to youth with the appeal of Hip-Hop. In addition, Chicago Pastor Phil Jackson has a designated church service for youth and young adults called "Tha House" and Christopher Martin of the popular Rap duo Kid N Play, who starred in the House Party movie sequels, founded Amen Films and produced a DVD entitled *Holy Hip-Hop*.

Within the same vein, but from a spiritual perspective, an underground song called "The Truth" approaches the issue from a non-religious standpoint. The song emphasizes acknowledging the Creator in truth and in doing and points out contradictions in the Bible. The word "controversial" may be an understatement due to the fact that the United States is a faith-based society, especially Black America. However, from a Hip-Hop argument, if we can accept creative radicalism from what is deemed 'gangsta rap,' then we should be open-minded enough to listen to a spiritual perspective, even if we don't necessarily agree with the philosophical beliefs of the artist. Nevertheless, it may be interesting and thought-provoking to examine some of the scriptures in question:

> II Samuel 6:23 vs. II Samuel 21:8
> Isaiah 37:1-38 vs. II Kings 19:1-37
> II Chronicles 36:9 vs. II Kings 24:8
> St. Matthew 1:6-16 vs. Luke 3:23-31

Mad Respect

Wyclef Jean, member of the hit-making Rap act The Fugees, was selected to serve as an Ambassador for his native country of Haiti. The Hip-Hop star used his position to advocate for many services for the Caribbean nation as well as to promote social and economic development through his organization, Yele Haiti Foundation, founded in 2005. The foundation offers scholarships, trains teachers, and builds schools. In addition, Wyclef launched Together for Haiti, a partnership to combat the food crisis in the country. Yele, which means "a cry for freedom," teamed with SolesUnited to distribute 10,000 pairs of recycled Crocs shoes. In addition, Wyclef seeks assistance for farmers in need and has received helped from other celebrities such as Matt Damon and Paul Simon.

You Don't Stop

The Smithsonian National Museum of American History in New York launched the *Hip Hop Won't Stop: The Beat, The Rhymes, The Life* exhibit in 2006. The exhibit recognizes and honors the pioneers of the art form that includes contributions from Ice T, Russell Simmons, Kool DJ Herc, and Grandmaster Flash. The museum's multi-year project traces Rap from its origins in the South Bronx in the 1970s to the present, paying homage to an art that generates nearly 500 billion dollars a year. The early struggles and rise of an art form that was once vilified and deemed a fad grew out of the imagination of America's most impoverished and disadvantaged people. What was cultivated from two turntables, simplistic rhymes, a distinguished and creative art, and acrobatic dance moves captivated the minds of millions of people around the world. Hip Hop won't stop.

The Message

The Rock and Roll Hall of Fame inducted the first Rap act, Grandmaster Flash and the Furious Five during its ceremony in 2007. The pioneering Rap act, whose hits include "Freedom," "Its Nasty," "The Message," "Scorpio," and "New York, New York," were honored for their groundbreaking work and contributions in Hip-Hop. The Furious Five included Kid Creole, Mele Mel, Scorpio, Rahiem and the late Keith Cowboy, along with DJ Grandmaster Flash are widely considered the most significant act in Hip-Hop history. Grandmaster Flash innovated the break beat on two turntables, Mele Mel created the rhyme cadence that 99% of all emcees use, Keith Cowboy invented the popular phrase "Throw your hands in the air and wave 'em around like you just don't care" and was the first emcee to master the call-and-response crowd interaction. The group created Hip-Hop's first live-stage performance and were the first stars of the musical genre years before records were made. Their 1982 hit "The Message" is noted as the first Rap song to cross over to the Pop charts.

How High

In 2007, Hip Hop made it to Capitol Hill in Washington DC for a hearing to address images and languages used in music. The hearing included rappers Master P, David Banner, and Hip-Hop Historian Michael Eric Dyson. Although the issues surrounded negative imagery and derogatory language, the fact that Rap music has a powerful-enough impact on society to be brought in front of the Energy and Commerce Subcommittee speaks volumes of an art form that was once decried a fad and largely discriminated against by the record industry.

Kingdom Come

Rap mega-star Jay-Z did done the unthinkable. What was once unfathomable of a Rap artist in terms of success from a historical perspective, has been achieved and, in many cases, surpassed. In 2007, the Rap superstar tied the Rock and Roll Legend Elvis Presley with 10 number 1 albums on the U.S. Pop Album Charts with the release of American Gangster. In 2009, Jay-Z released *The Blue Print 3*, surpassing Elvis who was then at the top spot as a solo artist with the most number 1 albums.

Jay-Z's Number 1 albums are:

- Reasonable Doubt
- In My lifetime, Vol. 1
- Vol. 2…Hard Knock Life
- Vol. 3…Life and Times of S. Carter
- The Dynasty: Roc La Familia
- The Blue Print
- The Blue Print 2: The Gift and the Curse
- The Black Album
- Kingdom Come
- American Gangster
- Blue Print 3

The Hip Hop Hall of Fame

The late Notorious B.I.G. and Tupac Shakur were honored as icons of Hip-Hop as they were inducted into the Hip-Hop Hall of Fame in 2002. They were joined in a class that included Afrika Bambaataa, LL Cool J, Queen Latifah, Run-DMC, Salt 'N Pepa, Slick Rick, and Doug E. Fresh. In addition, DJs Kool Herc and Grandmaster Flash, break-dancer Crazy Legs, Russell Simmons, and graffiti artist Dondi were inductees. The hall of fame induction was a precursor to the Hip-Hop Super Conference and Expo that included more than 100 panel discussions on Hip-Hop culture. The induction included pioneers of each era from the most innovative to the most creative, recognizing the diversity and genius of the multi-faceted art form.

The Making of History

The Library of Congress' National Recording Registry includes musical selections that are culturally, historically, or aesthetically significant. Their selections include some of the biggest names in music history. In 2002, pioneering Rap group Grandmaster Flash and the Furious Five were added to the names of legendary performers that include Sam Cook, Sarah Vaughn, and Bob Marley, to name a few. The Rap group's hit "The Message," a seven-minute commentary on ghetto life, was added to the Library's collection for the purpose of historical preservation. The song was released in 1982 and was reported as being certified gold within 18 days, selling over a half million copies and was in route to double-platinum status. The hook of the song, "Don't push me 'cause I'm close to the edge. I'm trying not to lose my head" is one of the most popular phrases in music history.

Cash Rules Everything Around Me

Rap music broke new ground in 2007. Forbes compiled its first-ever list of the richest rappers that included Jay-Z, who headed the list with $34 million dollars, followed by 50 Cent who earned 32 million dollars, and Diddy who earned 28 million dollars. Timbaland, Dr. Dre, Eminem, Snoop Dog, and Kanye West were also in the top ten. Their earnings were generated from album sales, investments, endorsements, and other business ventures.

Hot In Herre!

In 2002, Rap star Nelly released his second solo album *Nellyville* and set his career in overdrive. The album's first single, the Neptune-produced hit, "Hot In Herre," not only reached the number one spot on the singles chart, but made history for receiving more air play than any other song in the history of Rap and mainstream R&B. This funky sing-song dance hit holds another distinguished record for an audience of 163.1 million, the highest ever for any song during a one week period!

Bring The Noise

Mos Def received a ticket for performing outside of Radio City Music Hall in 2006. Mos Def, performing on the back of a flatbed truck, was cited by police for operating a sound device without a permit. The song "Katrina Clap," dedicated to the victims of the hurricane, was shut down early, but the message resonated among the thousands who gathered in attendance and cheered him on.

Hip Hop Is Dead?

Nas turned Hip-Hop on its ear with the controversial title of his album *Hip Hop Is Dead*. The statement generated numerous conversations among fans and artists alike, alluding to the declining record sales, waning popularity, along with mundane, profanity-laced themes of drugs, sex, and violence. A number of prominent luminaries weighed in on the subject from Chuck D to Michael Eric Dyson, among others. The title generated more conversation within Hip-Hop than any other issue since the onslaught of Gangsta Rap.

Brand New Funk

Will Smith is the first and most successful rapper to transition from music to acting and is perhaps the greatest Hip-Hop personality of all time. After starring in the hit television show *Fresh Prince of Bel Air*, Will took his acting talents to the silver screen and with a combination of charisma, charm, comedic wit, and for women sex appeal, he began to dominate Hollywood like very few before his time. In 1996, Will starred in the blockbuster hit *Independence Day*, which became the top box office grossing film of the year. By 2008, with the success of the movie *Hancock*, Will became the first Hollywood actor to star in ten consecutive movies to earn over 100 million dollars.

Can I Kick it?

February 24, 2002, Big Daddy Kane was on stage in front of a jam-packed crowd at the Isaac Hayes Club in Chicago. Kane, pimped out with a fur coat and hat, hit a fast-paced impromptu rhyme that warmed up the audience. As the beat slowed down to a steady bop, Kane started a flow and after a few bars, he dropped the mic and the music stopped abruptly. The house was silent and as Kane picked up the mic and dusted it off, the beat kicked back in and he finished his rhyme with, "drop shit and make it still look good" and the crowd erupted into total pandemonium!

Make Room for the Man

On May 2, 2008, Sean "Diddy" Combs was honored with a star on the Hollywood Walk of Fame during a ceremony in Los Angeles. The Hip-Hop mogul's contribution to the world of entertainment includes a string of classic, platinum and gold hits as both artist and producer and who's talent is behind the success of such notable acts as the Notorious B.I.G., Mase, and Mary J Blige, to name a few. In branching out to other areas of entertainment, Diddy co-starred in the critically acclaimed Broadway Revival of *A Raisin In the Sun*, a television adaptation, which aired in February 2008. Along with a number of successful business ventures, Diddy earned his place on the famous red carpet.

The Blue Print

USA, the television cable network, celebrates a character of the month throughout the year to honor celebrities for their various accomplishments. In the month of May, 2008 they honored Rap superstar Jay-Z. Jay-Z's impeccable resume includes eleven consecutive platinum and multi-platinum albums, a string of number one hits, and part ownership of the New Jersey Nets' NBA franchise as well as other business ventures to include a clothing line. Jay-Z is known as one of the most successful personalities in Hip-Hop history and his recognition by the USA network underscores his prominent stature in the world of entertainment.

Minds' Playin' Tricks On Me?

On Friday January 26, 2007, the city of Houston, Texas honored Rap-A-Lot Records CEO James Prince with his own day. James is credited for the emergence of Scar Face and the Geto Boys, who dominated the Rap game below the Mason Dixie Line before the South became 'Dirty.' In recognition of building a recreation center that will serve Houston's 5th Ward and other charitable work over the last 20 years, Houston officially proclaimed January 26th as "James Prince Day." The success of such artists as Scarface, Big Mike, Willie D, and the

Geto Boys, along with giving back to the community, is a testament to the genius of James Prince.

The Icon

In 2007, BET (Black Entertainment Television) named rapper KRS-One the recipient of it's I Am Hip-Hop Icon Award. The award recognizes and honors KRS-One's relentless commitment to uplifting and the preservation of Hip-Hop from his music to his ministry and social activism. As a young man, KRS-One was, at one point, homeless and against insurmountable odds, overcame his personal plight and circumstances through his love for music. His 1986 debut with the single "South Bronx" and the classic LP *Criminal Minded* as a member of Boogie Down Productions is the perfect example as to why the "Teacha'" stands as a temple in Hip-Hop.

Rolling

Rolling Stone, widely recognized as a leading authority and voice on Pop music and culture, recently released a list of the 500 greatest songs of all time. Their list includes some of the biggest names and icons in the history of the music industry. Artist such as Michael Jackson, The Beatles, Ray Charles, Diana Ross and the Supremes, and Marvin Gaye are just a few of the many legends mentioned. Needless to say, a number of Rap songs are represented on the list.

They include:

#475 "Sabotage" by The Beastie Boys
#440 "Push It" by Salt 'N Pepa
#419 "Nuthin' But a G Thang" by Dr. Dre
#417 "Fuck the Police" by NWA
#386 "I Know You Got Soul" by Eric B. and Rakim
#346 "California Love" by Tupac and Dr. Dre
#322 "Fight the Power" by Public Enemy
#287 "Walk This Way" by Run DMC
#248 "Rappers Delight" by Sugarhill Gang

#237 "Planet Rock" by Afrika Bambaataa and the Soul Sonic Force
#180 "Hey Ya!" by Outkast
#166 "Lose Yourself" by Eminem
#160 "Bring the Noise" by Public Enemy
#51 "The Message" by Grand Master Flash and the Furious Five

All Around the World Same Song

Rap artist Waterflow, one of Senegal's most famous Rap artists, has used his music to address the problems of his country. In Senegal, journalists are controlled by the government and are not able speak and write at freewill. During the 2000 election, the voice of Hip-Hop used its influence to change the political landscape of the country, resulting in a new regime. The music of Waterflow and other artists addresses the affliction of poverty, the lack of running water and electricity, and serves as motivation to the country's youth.

Hip Hop Hooray

Twelve

Rock Da House

Spit Fire

Hip-hop continues to grow in all aspects of the culture. An example is the 2007 debut of the Hip-Hop talk show *Spit Fire*. An extension of the portal www.IAmHipHop.com, *Spit Fire* is hosted by Rap legend Kool Mo Dee. The show delves into social, political, economic, and artistic expressions from a Hip-Hop perspective. Special guests are featured such as Chuck D, Grandmaster Mele Mel, Xibit, Tavis Smiley, DMC, and Doug E. Fresh, to name a few, and is taped in Los Angeles before a live studio audience.

Get Rich Or Die Tryin'

Rap superstar 50 Cent hit the Hip-Hop scene like none other. From a prison stint and gunshot wounds to beef with several other rappers, 50 Cent was destined for fame in some shape, form, or fashion. Thus, the release of his debut LP *Get Rich Or Die Tryin'* on February 6, 2003 made music history. Within five days, the album sold over 872,000 units, the best-selling debut album since Soundscan started its tracking system in 1991.

If You Don't Know, Now You Know

If you were to take a guess as to which rapper had the longest reign in the Rap game, most people would say L.L. Cool J. Although L.L. had an impressive run that began in 1984 with the single "I Need A

Beat," he doesn't have the longest reign in the game. That title belongs to the Oak Town emcee Too Short, who dropped his first album *Don't Stop Rappin'* in 1983. Too Short is still releasing jams to this day after a career spanning over 25 years, which includes an impressive string of gold, platinum and multi-platinum LPs.

Rappa Ternt Sanga

T-Pain is a hit-making, Grammy Award-winning singer, songwriter, and producer. He is widely popular for his electronic sounding vocals, a throw back to the late Roger TRap in the song "Computer Love." T-Pain released his debut single "I'm Sprung" in 2005 and his album, *Rappa Ternt Sanga,* in November of the same year. As his popularity as an artist has grown, T-Pain has done a number of collaborations with Mike Jones, Styles P., Akon, Bonecrusher, Ludacris, and Lil Wayne, to name a few. Amazingly, T-Pain has the most ring-tones ever sold.

Month In The Mix

The soft drink company Pepsi Co. created a DJ division that will celebrate the musical art for an entire month. August has been designated for showcasing the art of turntablism where events take place in various cities across the nation. Honoring DJs such as Grandmaster Flash, D.J. Jazzy Jeff, and others, the first event started out at the New York hotspot Arena and worked it's way to Atlanta, Chicago, Detroit, Los Angeles, Miami, St. Louis, and Washington, DC.

Hip-Hop Today and Back in the Day

The Los Angeles-based KDAY is known as the first Hip-Hop radio station ever. KDAY launched the careers of many West Coast rappers from the World Class Wrecking Cru to N.W.A. After going off the air for a period of time, KDAY returned in the summer of 2004 with the slogan "Hip-Hop Today and Back in the Day." Some of Cali's most popular DJs joined the show, including Rap artist Yo-Yo, who first gained popularity from collaborating with Ice Cube. Today, KDAY plays a variety of old school and current urban music on 93.5 FM.

Ruthless Records

Jerry Heller and Eazy-E co-founded Ruthless Records in 1987. The independent label put West Coast Rap on the map by launching the careers of Eazy-E and N.W.A. At the same time, Ruthless introduced Gangsta Rap to the music industry with songs like "Boyz N the Hood," a hardcore story of street tales written by Ice Cube and was later used as the title to John Singleton's movie. Ruthless released the gold single "Supersonic" by J.J. Fad along with the classics "Straight Outta Compton" and "Fuck Tha Police." In 2008, the label celebrated its 20th year anniversary.

Lollipop

Universal Music Group and Music Choice, an award-winning music network, announced the record-breaking success of Universal Motown Recording artist Lil' Wayne's "Lollipop" video on Music Choice. The video has been viewed an unprecedented one million times two weeks in a row. Lil' Wayne is the first artist ever to achieve this milestone since Video On Demand Music Network was launched in 2004. To celebrate Lil' Wayne's success, Music Choice produced a special original show entitled "Lil Wayne-A Milli."

The Hush Tour

The *Hush Tour*, which is a Hip-Hop road show tour of New York City, gives a detailed overview of the elements of Hip-Hop: the DJ, the MC, the B-Boy (Break dancer), and Graffiti Artists. The Hush Tour is hosted by the very legends who helped found the culture; Grandmaster Caz of the Cold Crush Brothers, Rahiem of Grandmaster Flash and the Furious Five, Kool DJ Herc, and DJ Red Alert are a few of the celebrity guides. The tour takes you to the actual locations from the Bronx to Harlem and the hot spots where Hip-Hop began. This tour is highly recommended for anyone who wants to know the true history of the culture.

Stand Up

In November of 2006, Sean Bell, an unarmed Black man was gunned down in a hail of bullets from undercover New York City police the night before his wedding. The incident, along with the acquittal of the officers involved, provoked a storm of protest lead by Civil Rghts activist the Reverend Al Sharpton. AllHipHop.com became involved in the movement with a collaboration of artists to include Swizz Beatz, Talib Kweli, and Cassidy, among others, in recording the song "Stand Up (A Sean Bell Tribute)." The money from the iTunes sales was donated to The Sean Bell Benefit Fund.

Tha Carter III

Tha Carter III is the title of the 6th LP from the New Orleans Rap superstar Lil' Wayne. The first release from the album is the chart-topping hit "Lollipop," the song that blazed the airwaves for months during the summer of 2008. The buzz about the album kicked off after several mixed tapes hit the streets and the momentum kept building until it damn-near exploded. Featuring guest appearances by T Pain, Robin Thicke, Busta Rhymes, and Jay-Z, the album sold 423,000 copies on the first day of its release and hit the 1 million mark within a week.

Graduation

Kanye West's *Graduation* dropped September 11, 2007 and posted the largest sales total in more than two years on the Billboard's 200. According to Nielson Soundscan, West's album moved 957,000 units in the first 6 days and ranked 15th among all sales weeks since Nielson Soundscan started tracking in 1991. The LP also set a record for digital downloads for a first week's release with 133,000.

Fresh Fest 2005

Blackberry Entertainment, Inc. hosted a concert in honor of old school Hip-Hop titled Fresh Fest 2005. The concert featured a host of legends to include Doug E Fresh, Slick Rick, Big Daddy Kane, Biz

Markie, Dana Dane, Nice and Smooth, Whodini, and the Sugarhill Gang. The artists reflected the 30-year history of Hip-Hop, where and how it originated and developed into what it is today. The event took place at the Hammerstein Ballroom in New York City on August 12, 2005 and is celebrated as the biggest old school concert ever.

8 Mile

On March 23, 2003, Eminem became the first Rap artist to win an Academy Award for Best Song with the hit "Lose Yourself" from the Hip-Hop movie *8 Mile*. The film is loosely based on his life as a struggling rapper from the streets of Detroit. It was a popular choice among the urban and Hip-Hop generations. "Lose Yourself" received the nod over "The Hands That Built America" by U2 from the movie *Gangs of New York*. The award marks a milestone not just for Eminem as an artist, but also for Rap music as a whole.

War Child

May 13, 2008 was the release date of the album *War Child*, an LP of autobiographical songs by the Sudanese child-soldier-turned-rapper Emmanuel Jal. As young as 8 years old, Jal fought in Sudan's Liberation Army using an A-K 47 riffle. Jal, now 28, relives his experiences in his songs "Forced To Sin" and "Shadows of Death" from his album. The global impact of Hip-Hop couldn't be more evident than with *War Child* and the influential power more prominent than the life of Emmanuel Jal.

Stronger

During the 2008 Gammy Awards show, Kanye West put on a stellar performance. The Rap superstar paid tribute to his late mother, Dr. Donda West, with a powerful performance of the song "Hey Momma." Wearing a light-up jacket and shades with a futuristic stage prop, Kanye dazzled the crowd with the song "Stronger" and the multi-Grammy Award winner shaved the word "Momma" into his hair in the back of his head.

Party Time

In June of 2005, Hip-Hop pioneer Kurtis Blow was inducted into the Bronx Wall of Fame. The Harlem native was recognized for his contributions in the early years of Hip-Hop as the art form flourished throughout the Bronx in the 1970s. And as a tribute in his honor, a "Kurtis Blow" street sign was unveiled at the Grand Concourse Bronx Supreme Court Building. Kurtis Blow gained fame with the hit songs "Christmas Rappin'," "The Breaks," and "If I Ruled the World."

Hip-Hop In the White House

Rosa Clemente is not only a Hip-Hop activist, but she was named as the vice presidential running mate of 2008's Green Party Presidential candidate Cynthia McKinney. Rosa has been active for a number of years presenting workshops and lectures at colleges, universities, high schools, and prisons. In 2003, she helped form and coordinate the first ever National Hip-Hop Political Convention. As a vice presidential candidate, Rosa was the first Hip-Hop personality with the opportunity to be voted into the White House.

Temple of Hip-Hop

KRS-ONE founded the Temple of Hip-Hop to preserve the culture of the art form. The Temple stands as an organization dedicated to changing the way government, media, religious, educational, and civic organizations understand and view Hip-Hop. The collective members of the Temple as a conscious body of "Hip-Hopas" balances Hip-Hop's image in world history. The aim is to be an active preservation society that inspires the Hip-Hop community to be a community.

Higher Learning

Howard University's Graduate School hosted the Hip-Hop & Higher Education Symposium on March 30, 2006. The event featured a number of guests and workshops that addressed Hip-Hop and its role in higher education. Bakari Kitwana, author of the book, "The Hip-Hop Generation: Why White Kids Love Hip-Hop," participated as a keynote speaker along with Melyssa Ford (BET VJ) and Hip-Hop artist Lil' Mo, to name a few. The event attracted hundreds of students and fans alike that were able to see the Hip-Hop culture from an intellectual perspective.

Notorious

Notorious is the title of the biopic about the Brooklyn-born Rap legend Notorious B.I.G. The release was slated for January 2009 through Fox Searchlight Pictures. The film chronicles Biggie's rise to stardom, his marriage with Faith Evans, and his struggles on the street before launching a successful Rap career. The soundtrack is loaded with his hit singles "Hypnotize," "Juicy," and "One More Chance," to name a few, along with unrecorded tracks from his early demos. Guest appearances on the soundtrack include a production from Kanye West, former Bad-Boy label mate Jay-Z on the cut "Brooklyn Go hard," Jadakiss with "A Letter to B.I.G.," and Faith Evans and his son, Christopher "CJ" Wallace Jr., performing on a new version of "One More Chance." The movie was highly anticipated and celebrates the life of a legend.

Whatever You Like

In 2008, T.I.'s hit "live Your Life," featuring Rihanna, took a nose-dive from #80 to #1 on Billboard's Hot 100, setting a new record for the biggest jump into the #1 spot in the chart's 50-year history. Additionally, T.I. is the first artist since Usher in 2004 to replace himself at #1 on the Hot 100 as "Live Your Life" knocked his first single "Whatever You Like" to #2. Both singles are from the album *Paper Trail*, which debuted at #1 on the Billboard 200 with the first week's sales close to 600,000—more copies than the next four albums on the chart combined.

> *I think all of the movies at that time had an impact. Wild Style was an incredible raw film on Hip-Hop. Then you had Beat Street and then Breakin'. Breakin' sold a lot of tickets in the theatres and then Krush Groove was very hot. It was me, Run-DMC, the Fat Boys, New Edition, and Sheila E. It was a hot, hot movie with a lot of stars in it.*
> —Kurtis Blow

The Mark of X

Mix gas and fertilizer
With 16 bars
Will blow the stage to the roof
And the roof to the stars
A-yo, I've been iconic
Since embryonic with topics
While verses disperse
Leaving scenes chaotic
Light the mind with ideas
'Til I'm glowing out the ears
So when I rhyme
I shift paradigms like gears
The only pro with a flow
Hard enough to crack a track
And when I die they'll clone
my DNA to bring me back
Yo, sentence after sentence
Whose rhyme can go the distance
You'll be met with maximum
Resistance in an instance
'Cause I write like a Shiite
On a mission for Jihad
Camouflage and fatigue
In a league meant for gods
Thoughts are so loaded
The ink pen exploded
Cross rappers like freight trains
And leave 'em railroaded
'Cause I flow like Niagara
While fake souljas stagger
Smack your wack track
And leave a dagger in your swagger

Yo, mic after mic
I keep 'em smoking like charcoal
With plush rhymes like
Italian Marble and artful
Like a pimped out style
That's how you know it's me
'Cause the word became flesh
And I became poetry

In 1983, Disco Fever was the Mecca of Hip-Hop. Sometimes I would have 30 recording artists in my club at the same time. That was unheard of, unprecedented. I don't think that ever happened in the history of music except for maybe Studio 54, and I still don't think that many people would be in Studio 54 at the same time, in the same night.
—Sal Abbatiello

Unfortunately, I think that Rap has stolen the term Hip-Hop from the culture. I do not believe that Rap is Hip-Hop. It's one element of Hip-Hop. Back when that move was made of stealing the term Hip-Hop and applying it to Rap to the exclusion of b-boying, turntablism, deejaying, fashion, and graffiti, Hip-Hop died. At the exclusion of the other disciplines, Rap, in a way, killed Hip-Hop, which was done back in the 90s. The other elements didn't die, but Hip-Hop, as a cohesive culture, died when all of its facets separated from each other and went on their own. So Hip-Hop is dead.
—Michael Holman

Hip Hop Hooray

Hall of Fame Hits

"AWARD TOUR"—A TRIBE CALLED QUEST

"WIKKA RAP"—THE EVASIONS

"PAPARAZZI"—XZIBIT

"SUPERSTAR"—LUPE FIASCO

"GAMES PEOPLE PLAY"—SWEET GEE

"GET BY"—TALIB KWELI

"SMURFIES DANCE"—SPYDER D

"MAGIC STICK"—50 CENT FEATURING LIL' KIM

"HEY YOUNG WORLD"—SLICK RICK

"I'LL BE THERE FOR YOU"—METHOD MAN FEATURING MARY J. BLIGE

"THE BOSS"—RICK ROSS

"IT'S YOURS"—T LA ROCK AND DJ JAZZY JAY

"BANG ZOOM (LET'S GO-GO)"—THE REAL ROXANNE

"NOW THAT WE FOUND LOVE"—HEAVY D AND THE BOYZ

Thirteen

Getting Jiggy Wit It

Interview with Kaneri Diamond

Q. Who were the artists that influenced you when you were coming up in hip-Hop?

A. The artist that really made me want to know more about Hip-Hop is Tupac when he came out with "Brenda's Got A Baby." Being in Florida at that time, I think that song opened up a lot of kid's minds. It struck up a little controversy in Florida and that's when I started to like Hip-Hop.

Q. I know some of your label mates, Rick Ross, Trina, and Plies. Are they featured on your album coming out?

A. No. I'm going in a different direction. I'm not trying to have a lot of features on my album. It's nothing against features, I just want everyone to know who Kaneri Diamond is. I'm trying to bring it back to the real essence of Hip-Hop. Hip-Hop right now is a little sleep to me and I don't listen to a lot of music out right now because I don't want it to clutter my creativity. I like Outkast, Andre 3000, Kanye West, and the Roots, Lauryn Hill—she's probably influenced me with my music more than anybody else. It's so many rappers that put out songs with the message "Go on the corner and sell drugs" or "Pick up a gun and kill somebody." That's the wrong message to give to the youth because they really look up to these rappers and really think these rappers are living these lives. A lot of brothers get caught up in the situation and end up with a long term in prison trying to follow a Rap song.

Q. Did you film a video for your single "Like This?"

A. Actually, I'm going with another single right now called "Mo' Money."

Q. What would you say is your greatest moment in Hip-Hop?

A. I remember when India Arie came out. She was more like neo-soul, but her music was so powerful. When she came out, I went out and bought a guitar and tried to teach myself how to play because of what she was doing, the message that she was bringing, and how she inspired me. I've been around a lot of big artists, partying and doing different types of events, but it wasn't anything great because I think greatness comes with change.

Q. When I think of Hip-Hop in Florida, the first name that jumps to mind is Luke and the 2 Live Crew and the 69 Boys. Were they a huge impact on popularizing Hip-Hop in Florida?

A. You can't be from Florida and not know Uncle Luke, 2 Live Crew and the 69 Boys with the "Tootsie Roll." We 'rolled' it up for years. In this particular market, we like to dance like popping and locking and those particular artists, they influenced those types of dance moves. You know, JZ Money and Trick Daddy, they opened the doors for a lot of artists in Florida coming out right now.

Q. What are your long-term goals as an artist?

A. I want to own my own company, an entertainment company, or record label. I want to own my own clothing line (I'm very much into fashion) and branch out into acting. I want to take it to the limit. I want to do shows, reality T.V. and take it to the limit. I want to do some positive things with teenage kids and do something good in the community.

Q. If you had to describe your music in a few words what would it be?

A. Superflylistic

Queen Pen

Q. What types of projects are you currently working on?

A. I have my program for domestic violence, a foundation for children.

You know, Hip-Hop now is not about doing a whole album. I tell people everything comes back. Everything before comes back. You do that one record, send it in to stations, and see what happens from there. So, I'm more-so concentrating on getting that club record 'cause then I can make my money off of shows and you don't need the big labels for that and continuing recording, recording, and recording and putting records out there and see what happens from there. That's where Hip-Hop is right now. It's about getting that record out there—getting that buzz—and it's about making your own money and not depending on labels giving you that $0.98 a record.

Q. How did you start out as an artist?

A. Teddy gave me my first entry into the game. "No Diggity," that song was a big hit and it changed my whole life. It came right on time.

Q. What are your current plans?

A. We're going overseas in March (Black Street). Overseas is a place where Hip-Hop is really appreciated. It's a different appreciation over here. Their fan-base, they don't easily let go as they do in America. They don't change with the fad. People over there, they give love to new artists in the game, but they also still hold on to that love for the ones that came before, you know, whoever was hot back at that time. So you can be an artist like Das Efx and go over there and make money. You can be an artist that was out before who made some hits and go over there and make money. That fan base over there is solid.

Q. Who were the artists that influenced you when you were coming up in Hip-Hop?

A. Eric B and Rakim. I loved Eric B and Rakim, Salt 'N Pepa, MC Lyte, Queen Latifah, and even though she wasn't Hip-Hop, I loved Tina Turner. She was just a woman who went through high hell and water and I was like, "Damn! That's me!" So it wasn't just Hip-Hop. I loved Billy Holiday.

Q. How do you feel about the female presence in Hip-Hop now?

A. No presence, there is no presence. Look at every female that's been in Hip-Hop—she's always had that hot, male, Hip-Hop artist to stand behind: Lil Kim; Biggie, Brat; Jermaine Dupree. Everybody had a hot male, which means we never had our own identity. Not saying the women I just named wasn't dope, but those women never got to shine on their own. I don't think that Hip-Hop is used to seeing females on their own. A dude can come back after a hiatus at 42 years old and he's accepted. A chick comes back in her early 30's and she's old, she needs to stop it.

Q. How did you like working with Teddy Riley?

A. It was one of the best experiences I've had as an artist. Teddy is a beast at what he does. Teddy also made me the person that I am now when I go into the studio now and I'm so used to working with Teddy, it's hard to work with other producers. It's hard because he's a perfectionist.

Q. What is your favorite moment in Hip-Hip?

A. My favorite moment is when Obama was elected President.

*Its so many rappers that put out songs with the message
'go on the corner and sell drugs or pick up a gun and kill
somebody.' That's the wrong message to give to the youth
because they really look up to these rappers and really think
these rappers are living these lives. A lot of brothers get
caught up in the situation and end up with a long term in
prison trying to follow a Rap song.*
—Kaneri Diamond

Rosa Clemente

Q. I'm familiar with your work as an activist as well as your presence within the culture, but for the benefit of our readers, can you give a brief background of how you started out as an activist?

A. I started out when I was an undergrad at the Sate University of New York at Albany. My second year after I switched my major to Africana Studies, I got to be President of the Albany State University Black Alliance (SUBA) it's one of the oldest Black/African-decent student unions in the state of New York. So, it just happened that there was an opening and some people asked me to run and I did. That really began my activism really on my college campus.

Q. In terms of our community—and I'm referring to people of color—we have a lot of issues we need to address from education and unemployment to poverty and imprisonment. Do you feel that Rap artists and professional athletes should share in the responsibility of uplifting our communities, if so, how?

A. I think those problems really come out of structural racism and white supremacy in this country. I think that people who have power, the have the ultimate responsibility of dealing with the societal issues that a lot of young people of color find themselves in. Artists and sports people-my take on that is like what Paul Roberson said that every artist has a responsibility-the ultimate responsibility. These people are multi-millionaires who are capitalist. I don't look to them to have a responsibility, they should, but for the most part, they don't and I think we waste a lot of time asking them to care when some of them just don't care. That's how I see it.

Q. If you had the opportunity to speak with the current Rap stars of today, like artists 50 Cent and G Unit, Young Jeezy, Snoop Dog, and T.I., what would you say to them about their music?

A. Well, I don't listen to them. I don't listen to 50 Cent. I listen to T.I. I think T.I. has a better understanding of politics in the world. That, to me, is not like most of my reality. I listen to it because I want to hear what young people are saying. For the most part, they're rappers. They're people who perform and people who make a lot of money to perform. I don't have an opinion on, "are they horrible"? "Is it good rap? Is it bad rap? Is it non-conscious, conscious? I can't put stuff into those categories. I expect them to act like grown men that they are, but they don't even do that at 36 and 37. I'm more at the other end of just, like, understanding where they come from and listening to stuff so I'll know where the young people are coming from and not having them as a main thing that I deal with. I don't like to judge people.

Q. Music is my first love, but I also enjoy reading books like the *Autobiography of Malcolm X*, *Nile Valley Contributions to Civilization* by Tony Browder, and a host of books from scholars such as Dr. Ben, Na'im Akbar, John Henrik Clarke, John G. Jackson, and Ivan Van Sertima. What are your favorite books and which ones would you recommend for young Hip-Hoppers who are thinking about activism?

A. I would definitely recommend the *Autobiography of Malcolm X*, *the Destruction of Black Civilization* by Dr. Chancellor Williams, *How Europe Underdeveloped Africa* by Walter Rodney, anything on Cointelpro and the Black poets of the 1960s.

Q. Who influenced you in Hip-Hop?

A. No one thing or person in particular, but being born in the South Bronx, I was brought up in Hip-Hop and listened to everybody that was out.

Q. How will the Hip-Hop community benefit from the Green Party?

A. The question is actually flipped. The Hip-Hop community can benefit from the Green Party, but the Green Party can benefit more from the Hip-Hop community and, hopefully, continue to build a bridge that will allow them to work together.

My greatest moment in Hip-Hop had to be the Tom Joyner Cruise 2010. Mr. Joyner dedicated a night to Hip-Hop and the show was called "Back to Black." The show was filled with Hip-Hop legends…Biz Markie, Common, Doug E. Fresh, Arrested Development, EPMD, Monie Love, Roxanne Shanté, The Fat Boys, Naughty By Nature, DJ Kool, DJ Scratch. Minister Farrakhan came out and gave everyone on the stage a charge to be responsible with our lyrics and he spoke on how we have so much POWER to change the world. Minister Farrakhan ended his Speech by giving all of us love and a special shout out to ARRESTED DEVELOPMENT. WOW, what a moment! I'll never forget that as long as I live!

—Eshe, Arrested Development

New World Order

Some suggest that I use
3 mics at a time
To sustain the high level
Of pressure from my rhymes
As if they were grown
And smuggled out of Colombia
One hit had you so high
You thought heaven was under ya'
Pack crowds by thousands
So heated when I'm performing
Ecologically it might
Explain global warming
When it comes to a battle
Line 'em up, I'll do 'em all
Ten minutes for twenty
Then spray the stage with luminal
From Roman empires
To ancient Aztec
The Great Wall of China
My mic, Heremeket
On the floor giving hips
Side effects like hydroxyphen
And while you bounce
You need my rhymes like oxygen
'Cause its necessary
More than extraordinary
Lyrically legendary
Mercenary to adversaries
'Cause had I lived
Two thousand years ago
And wrote rhymes on papyrus
I would've been a pharaoh

My Greatest moment in Hip-Hop is the moment that me and the Ladies play for the first time in #63 school yard on Boston Road in the Bronx. We had to carry our own equipment and records, then set up for mic. Check. We were nervous that day, but all those rehearsals paid off. We had excellent teachers (L brothers).

—Renee (Mercedes Ladies)

"There were many great moments, but listening to the radio and hearing Mr. Magic acknowledge me as a member of the Juice Crew!"

—Vaughn Cool V Lee

My greatest moment in Hip-Hop was when we became The Fearless 4. We signed with Enjoy Records then became the first Rap group to sign with a major label because of my cuz' Kurtis Blow became friends with Mr. Magic and doing Radio City's first Rap show with Kurtis Blow, .Run DMC, and Jam Master Jay, Rock Steady Crew, UTFO, and Fat Boys."

—The Great Peso (Fearless 4)

Hall of Fame Hits

"SLIPPIN'" -DMX

"HOW YA LIKE ME NOW?"—KOOL MOE DEE

"DEAR MOMMA"—2 PAC

"GOLD DIGGER"—KANYE WEST FEATURING JAMIE FOXX

"THA CROSSROADS"—BONE THUGS-N-HARMONY

"IT TAKES TWO"—ROB BASE & DJ EZ ROCK

"THE ROOF IS ON FIRE"—ROCK MASTER SCOTT & THE DYNAMIC 3

"THE POWER"—SNAP

"RAPPER'S DELIGHT"—SUGARHILL GANG

"PUSH IT"—SALT N PEPA

"WILD THING"—TONE LOC

"THE BREAKS"—KURTIS BLOW

"ICE ICE BABY"—VANILLA ICE

"THE MESSAGE"—GRANDMASTER FLASH & THE FURIOUS 5

Fourteen

Notable Hip Hop Work

"C.R.E.A.M."—WU TANG CLAN

"Cash rules everything around me," remember that? What more can you say about Wu Tang? They were the first Rap crew I heard that had no weak link since the legendary Crash Crew. In fact, both groups have a number of similarities between the two of them and tight lyrical skills is the most prominent.

"GIN AND JUICE"—SNOOP DOGGY DOG

This is just one of many classic hits that Snoop and Dré have dropped over the years. "Gin and Juice" took the two of them over the top and they have been a dominating force in Hip-Hop ever since.

"A GOOD DAY"—ICE CUBE

Ice Cube has released a number of hits over his 20-year career in the game beginning with N.W.A. and later as a solo artist. However, Ice Cube never needed radio play to survive and thrive in the Rap game. "A Good Day" is probably his most successful work in terms of commercial appeal. This is why it is so significant as one of the top 100 greatest Rap hits.

"MR. BIG STUFF"—HEAVY D AND THE BOYZ

This is the song that put Heavy D. on the map. Everybody remembers this jam from back in the day and if you followed Heavy's, career you saw him evolve over the years as an artist, but this song was the launching pad.

"BIG POPPA"—NOTORIOUS B.I.G.

"I love it when you call me Big Poppa!" Biggie is the greatest flower the game has ever seen. The way he could string along his rhymes sentence after sentence is just unbelievable. Biggie had a stellar career and, like a lot of fans, I just wish he would've been around longer to drop more jams.

"U.N.I.T.Y."—QUEEN LATIFAH

Queen Latifah did for female artists what Will Smith did for the fellas in the Rap game—she became a mega Hip-Hop star. Queen Latifah elevated Hip-Hop with her success as an artist and actress by starring in block-buster hits like *Set It Off* (my favorite) and *Beauty Shop*, to name a few.

"ADVENTURES OF GRANDMASTER FLASH ON THE WHEELS OF STEEL"—GRANDMASTER FLASH & THE FURIOUS 5

This is a legendary piece of work. It is the first jam that highlights a D.J. on the wheels of steel, mixing various records, and keeping the beat going without a flaw. This is one of the reasons Grandmaster Flash is a legend in the game.

"A NIGHTMARE ON MY STREET"—DJ JAZZY JEFF & THE FRESH PRINCE

One of the first songs to crossover to the Pop charts and receive mainstream success, "A Nightmare On My Street" opened doors for Rap artists when Hip-Hop was, essentially, limited to Black radio. It also helped to put D.J. Jazzy Jeff and the Fresh Prince in the spotlight.

"SOUL SURVIVOR"—YOUNG JEEZY

Young Jeezy put it down and separated himself from the rest of the pack with "Soul Survivor," a platinum single and chart topper. If this jam is any indication of what he can do, we may be in for something special over the next several years.

"WHOOP THERE IT IS"—TAG TEAM

This is one of the best Hip-Hop jams to pack a dance floor and I would venture to say that it's one of the most popular Miami-based style hits ever.

"ONE LOVE"—WHODINI

"One Love" is the first Rap hit about the subject of love. This is very significant because Rap music has always had a street edge and element and this is what's so impressive about Whodini's work. Whodini created songs while most Rap acts only knew how to create rhymes. They could take a subject and format verses and tie it all together with a catchy hook. They were able to do this better than anyone else in the game, which is why they have a string of mega hits that continue to play on urban radio stations today.

"WHAT A MAN"—SALT 'N PEPA

Salt 'N Pepa set the stage for women in Hip-Hop once they received the torch that was passed along to them from The Sequence, the first established female Rap group in the industry. Sequence took Rap for women as far as it could go during the nascent years in Hip-Hop, but when Salt 'N Pepa hit the scene with more bountiful opportunities, they raised the bar and set the tone for every female artist that followed.

"HIP-HOP HOORAY"—NAUGHTY BY NATURE

Absolutely one of my favorite groups of all time. Naughty By Nature had a feel for making music and a creative knack for hits. Treach, one of the most fierce emcees in the history of the game, led the way with rough, colorful, lyrics and sing-along hooks that made jams like "Hip-Hop Hooray" a classic. This is why the title of this book is what it is.

"A FLY GIRL"—THE BOOGIE BOYS

The Boogie Boys rocked the summer of '85 with this classic joint. This is when I knew that Romeo J.D. of the group was one of the best and most underrated rappers in the game. If you ever get a chance to go back and listen to their albums, check out Romeo J.D.'s verses in songs like "Girl Talk," "You Ain't Fresh," "Run It," and "Pit Bull." The versatility is there, the delivery is there, and the lyrics are off the chain.

"LOOKING FOR THE PERFECT BEAT"—AFRIKA BAMBAATAA & THE SOUL SONIC FORCE

Afrika Bambaataa is one of the founding fathers of Hip-Hop. Through Hip-Hop, Bambaataa has transformed the lives of thousands of Black and Latino youths and the establishment of the Zulu Nation has been the most significant pillar in the Hip-Hop community since day one. In 2005, a street was named in his honor.

"FEAR OF A BLACK PLANET"—Public Enemy

Public Enemy is definitely a powerful presence when you look at the history of Hip-Hop. P.E. was the voice of the Black community and represented racial pride, social awareness, and self-responsibility. Their music helped to awaken thousands of minds and changed their lives for the better. They were a musical extension of the Black Power Movement and it would be unthinkable to imagine what Hip-Hop might be without them!

"WHITE LINES"—MELLE MEL

"White Lines" marked the solo career of Melle Mel, who is, hands down, the greatest emcee ever! The heat that Mel had from '78 through '85 was unbelievable. You had to be there to witness it. Before Rap was even accepted as an art form, Mel was sought after by R&B artists like Chaka Khan. Harry Bellefonte went after Mel to perform in the movie *Beat Street*; Miami Vice's TV show requested him; Dexter King recruited him to write and perform for the King Holiday project' and Quincy Jones went after Mel for his album *Back On The Block*. I have never witnessed another emcee in such high demand as Melle Mel and I'm not just referring to guest appearances on someone else's song, but for historical projects!

"THE ROOF IS ON FIRE"—ROCK MASTER SCOTT & THE DYNAMIC 3

A Hip-Hop classic that you could spin at a party right now and have the place jumping with everybody singing the hook, "The roof, the roof, the roof is on fire!

We don't need no water, let the mother #@* burn!"

"I NEED LOVE"—LL COOL J

A masterpiece is all you can say about this work. What LL did with love was an incredible feat. The poetic artistry in the lyrics along with a sensual delivery took this jam over the top. Lyrically and conceptually, it is one of the greatest Rap songs ever made.

"WHAT PEOPLE DO FOR MONEY"—DIVINE SOUNDS

Brooklyn-based trio Divine Sounds scored a monster hit with this jam. This was followed up with the joint "Changes" and the b-side "Bed Sty (Do Or Die)". Their career was short-lived, but I really liked the few jams they put out. Their last song that I remember was "How Fast Money Goes" and I thought it was a pretty decent jam. It received marginal air play on the radio, but they never quite hit like they did with "What People Do For Money."

"FRIENDS"—WHODINI

"Friends is a word we use everyday
Most of the time we use it in the wrong way
Now you can look the word up again and again
But the dictionary doesn't know the meaning of friends"

I remember reading an article on Whodini back in '85 and I was amazed by how Jalil explained how he wrote this song. The first verse was about friends in general, "We like to be with some because their funny, others come around when they need some money. Some you grew up with around the way and you're still real close to this very day."

The second verse was about a relationship and moving too fast before you really know each other. The last verse is about the friends that back stab. The thought and effort that went into this song was amazing. When you listen to most songs today, you can literally exchange the rhymes from one verse to another and this is because most rappers only know how to rhyme, but they don't know how to construct an actual song. This is one of the reasons why Whodini stands out as one of the best ever.

"CHRISTMAS RAPPIN'"—KURTIS BLOW

"Christmas Rappin'" was the second biggest hit for Rap music. It followed the huge success of "Rapper's Delight" and put Kurtis Blow's name on the map. It was the starting point for a long and prosperous career. Kurtis became the first artist to sign with a major label and his success opened the doors for others to do the same.

"U CAN'T TOUCH THIS"—MC HAMMER

A cover of Rick James' hit "Super Freak," "U Can't Touch This" is a monumental piece of work. From a commercial standpoint and as a crossover hit, this is the Rap song that I would venture to say has made the biggest impact in the history of the recording industry. Of course, Run DMC's "Walk This Way" was the first major crossover hit, but "U Can't Touch This" had more mainstream appeal when you talk about radio airplay, chart position, award recognition, and the mass media that covered Hammer following the song's success.

"THE MESSAGE"—GRANDMASTER FLASH & THE FURIOUS 5

> "A child is born with no state of mind
> Blind to the ways of mankind
> God is smiling on you, but He's frowning too
> Because only God knows what you'll go through."

This is undoubtedly the greatest song in the history of Hip-Hop! In fact,

"The Message" was inducted into the Library of Congress' National Recording Registry for historical preservation in 2002! This is one of many reasons why Mele Mel is the greatest MC of all time!

My greatest moment in Hip-Hop is when the scratch was created. Why? Because there is no Hip-Hop without it.
— Grand Wizard Theodore

Spit Fire

From the mind thoughts travel
At the speed of light
Creativity ensues
And then moves in flight
Brain cells activate
To the point of overload
So either rhyme
Or the cerebral cortex
Will explode
Yo, a god on the mic.
With a shine that's fluorescent
That'll highlight my status
As the baddest with a presence
Never before seen
And could never be equal
As if the Dead Sea Scrolls
Could ever have a sequel
From the mic. to your ear
To your brain to your conscious
To your facial expression
That says this shit is monstrous
The poppy never sloppy
But print like Hewlett Packard
So far ahead of one
You'd have to start counting backwards
Causing damage like earthquakes
Hurricanes and twisters
Touch the mic. after me
Will leave your hands with blisters
Around the world
Asante Sana and mucho gracias
For a style like Armani
As sharp as Versace is

With rhymes like Sanskrit
Under Shaolin wisdom
Flowing like my wind pipe
Was an irrigation system
In foreign lands, my mic. would be
Sacred as a calf
On a scale of 1 to 10
I'm a hundred and a half

Big Boi Aka Sir Lucious Left Foot

Big Boi from Outkast headlined a nationwide tour of his highly anticipated solo album, *Sir Lucious Left Foot: The Son of Chico Dusty.* Starting August 26, 2010 in Atlanta, Georgia, Big Boi performed hits from his debut solo LP as well as classic material from Outkasts' hits. The tour schedule was as follows:

Aug. 26 Atlanta, GA
Verizon Wireless Amphitheater

Sept. 2 Iowa City, IA
University of Iowa

Sept. 4 Atlanta, GA
Heineken Red Star Soul

Sept. 5 Atlantic City, NJ
Casbah

Sept. 6 New York, NY
Brooklyn Bowl

Sept. 17 Chicago, IL
Congress Theater

Sept. 18 Providence, RI
Brown University

Sept. 22 Arcata, CA
Arcata Community Center

Sept. 24 Las Vegas, NV
The Palms Casino

Notable Hip Hop Work

Sept. 25 Fontana, CA
Epicenter

Sept. 28 Atlanta, GA
The Tabernacle

Oct. 1 Bloomington, IN
Indiana University

Oct. 8 Columbia, SC
University of South Carolina

Oct. 15 San Diego, CA
UC of San Diego

Oct. 23 Seattle, WA
Show Box Sodo

Oct. 28 Charleston, SC
Charleston Visitors Center

Oct. 29 Asheville, NC
Asheville Civic Center (Moog Fest)

Oct. 30 Houston, TX
Tom Bass Park Amphitheater

Nov. 12 Chattanooga, TN
University of Tennessee at Chattanooga

Nov. 18 Sydney, Australia
Fox Studios

The Main Event
LETS GET READY TO R-U-M-B-L-E!!

As soon as the bell goes "ding dong" I bring strong
Flows like blows, so don't step in the ring wrong
And put up your guard and come hard 'cause I'm hittin'
To knock your ass through the ropes and have you spittin'
Your mouth piece out as I connect to the jaw
With a right and a left just like a south paw
Quick combinations, body blows, and head shots
Enough to leave the canvas with stains of red spots
Lyrical jabs, uppercuts, and a hook
Blow after blow, one round is all it took
To feel the power of the rhymes that I'm landin'
When it's over, we'll see who's the last man standin'
(hook)
My rhymes are like the times of Ali's ropey dope
It'll cut off the ring and put you on the ropes
I hope you don't think your corner men can coach you
Have 'em ready to throw the towel in when I approach you
With a flurry that leaves your vision blurry and it's trouble
When each rhyme can hit you two times you're seeing double
As a blow to your chin makes your head spin and when
You least expect it, it's connected once again
Then I switch up the flow and if the bell doesn't save ya'
Your knees are gonna' buckle from the blows I gave ya'
The points pile up, but score cards couldn't measure
How a top contender can surrender from the pressure
(hook)
Toe-to-toe, blow-for-blow as the knuckles exchange
But after the mic check, you'll buckle from mid range
Jabs to the temple, chin, and midsection
And power punches comin' from every direction
As I stick and move, as I weave and bob
How I'm quick to prove how I leave a job
Flat on your back stretched out in a daze
And you wonder what happened when you look up and gaze
At me on the mic, the referee countin'
The crowd screamin' loud as the tension is mountin'
But it's not the punch, it's how you receive it
And it's not how you come to the ring, it's how you leave it

Notable Hip Hop Work

Break Beats: A list of the early recordings that started the deejay movement

"Give It Up Or Turn It Loose"—James Brown

"Apache"—Incredible Bongo Band

"Goode Ole Music"—Funkadelic

"I know You Got Soul"—Bobby Byrd

"Dance To The Drummer's Beat"—Herman Kelly & Life

"Ain't No Half Steppin'"—Heat Wave

"Rock Steady"—Aretha Franklin

"Trans-Europe Express"—Kraftwerk

"Catch A Groove"—Juice

"Say It Loud, I'm Black and I'm Proud"—James Brown

"Get Into Something"—The Isley Brothers

"Take Me To The Mardi Gras"—Bob James

"The Mexican"—Babe Ruth

"Hot Shot"—Karen Young

"Get Up And Dance"—Freedom

"Jam On The Groove"—Ralph McDonald

"Scratchin'"—Magic Disco Machine

"Stand—Sly and the Family Stone

"Good Times"—Chic

Hall of Fame Hits

"JUMP"—KRISS KROSS

"PARENTS JUST DON'T UNDERSTAND"—DJ JAZZY JEFF & THE FRESH PRINCE

"ROXANNE, ROXANNE"—UTFO

"FREAKS COME OUT AT NIGHT"—WHODINI

"I NEED LOVE"—LL COOL J

"WHAT PEOPLE DO FOR MONEY"—DIVINE SOUNDS

"REQUEST LINE"—ROCK MASTER SCOTT & THE DYNAMIC 3

"THE SHOW"—DOUG E FRESH & THE GET FRESH CREW

"FRIENDS"—WHODINI

"SUMMER TIME"—DJ JAZZY JEFF & THE FRESH PRINCE

"CHRISTMAS RAPPIN'"—KURTIS BLOW

"U CAN'T TOUCH THIS"—MC HAMMER

"WALK THIS WAY"—RUN-DMC

"PLANET ROCK"—AFRIKA BAMBAATAA & THE SOUL SONIC FORCE

The Afterword

From 1990 to 2010 were decades of highs and lows and new adventures for Rap music. We saw the dominance of the West Coast in the early 90s with artists like Ice Cube embarking on a solo career, Dr. Dre, the D.O.C., and Snoop Dog, among others, shifting the power from its East Coast counterparts and New York roots. Naughty By Nature was one of the only East Coast crews representing at this time and they were from Jersey. However, Wu-Tang, Biggie, Nas, Jay-Z and Busta Rhymes eventually brought an equal balance to the game by the mid 90s. At the same time, artists from all over the country were now coming out and hitting the scene and Hip-Hop became multi-regional.

Rap had grown so large that Atlanta became a big venue with Jermaine Dupree producing hits for artists such as Kriss Kross, Da Brat, and Bow Wow. Cleveland had Bone Thugs-N-Harmony, Chi-town had Common and Twista, and Nelly represented St. Louis. Master P. and the Big Tymers (Cash Money Millionaires) were from New Orleans, Scar Face and the Geto Boys represented Houston, Eminem was from Detroit, and the Neptunes and Missy Elliot put Virginia on the map. At the same time, Philly was already down with D.J. Jazzy Jeff and the Fresh Prince and Florida with the 2 Live Crew. This diversity gave Rap a new platform with a variety of sounds and styles.

A low point in Hip-Hop took place during the mid-to-late '80s and into the early 2000s with the deaths of several top artists. Tupac, the crowned prince of poetry, passed away and shortly afterwards Biggie, the all-time flow master, met an untimely death. Big Pun and Jam Master Jay of Run DMC were also lost from the game. Over the years, Hip-Hop has witnessed the passing of many talented brothers and sisters who left their mark on the art from Buffy the Human Beat Box, Eazy-E, Scott La Rock, and M.C. Trouble to Keith Cowboy, Master Don, Trouble T-Roy, O.D.B., and other members of the Hip-Hop nation who are gone but not forgotten. We say, "Peace!"

In many ways, Hip-Hop has triumphed from its humble beginnings. M.C. Hammer became the first of a few artists to surpass platinum status and reach the Diamond mark by selling over ten million copies with his LP, *Please Hammer Don't Hurt 'Em*. He was joined in this elite class by Vanilla Ice, Eminem, and Out Kast. Meanwhile, Will Smith, LL Cool J, Queen Latifah, Bow Wow, and Ice Cube have starred in major motion pictures from *Men-In-Black* and *XXX State of the Union* to *Set It Off*, *S.W.A.T.* and *Roll Bounce*. This followed the successful and popular sitcoms *In The House*, *Living Single* and *Fresh Prince of Bel Air*.

Nelly surpassed 23 million sales with just seven albums, 50 Cent's LP *Get Rich Or Die Tryin'* broke the record for first week's sales of any major label debut in the entire Soundscan era, and Jay-Z became the first Rap artist to record eleven consecutive platinum albums. Kanye West set a record for multiple Grammy Award nominations in two years for the LPs *The College Dropout* and *Late Registration* and DMX was the first artist to debut at number one on the Billboard Pop Charts with his first five albums. His 6th album, *Year of the Dog*, barely missed the top spot and came in at number two. T.I., Young Joc, Lil' Wayne, and Birdman are all blazing right now along with Ludacris and Lloyd Banks, so the game is still in good hands.

Over the years, Rap has broken down barriers and etched itself into mainstream America against insurmountable odds. There was a time when Rap artists couldn't get deals from major labels or receive airplay during prime time on the radio. It took roughly five years for rappers

The Afterword

to have the opportunity to make albums. Despite all the odds and obstacles from being a "fad" to "inciting violence," Hip-Hop has maintained its ground and is here to stay. There is no telling what the future holds for Hip-Hop but for now *Idlewild* is playing in the movie theatres and Jay-Z has returned with the new CDs *Kingdom Come* and *Blue Print 3*. You never know what might be next!

Peace

Hip Hop Hooray

About the Author

Sean XLG Mitchell is the ultimate hip-hop griot. The Washington, DC native began his career with Foxy 99 FM in Fayetteville, North Carolina promoting platinum hit makers from Rockmaster Scott and the Dynamic Three to M.C. Hammer.

Sean XLG is the first rap artist to win a national music competition. He currently works as a freelance writer and is the creator of the hip-hop category *Adult Contemporary Rap*.

ORDER FORM
WWW.AMBERBOOKS.COM

Fax Orders: 480-283-0991
Telephone Orders: 602-743-7211
Postal Orders: Send Checks & Money Orders to:
    Amber Books
    1334 E. Chandler Blvd., Suite 5-D67, Phoenix, AZ 85048
Online Orders: E-mail: Amberbk@aol.com

____*Hip Hop Hooray: Celebrating 30 Years of Rap Music*, ISBN #: 978-1-937269-15-9, $15.00
____*Lil Wayne: An Unauthorized Biography*, ISBN #: 978-0-09-824922-2, $15.00
____*God Made Dirt: The Life & Times of Ol' Dirty Bastard*, ISBN 978-0-9824922-2-2, $16.95
____*Prince in the Studio (1975-1995)*, ISBN #: 979-0-9790976-6-9, $16.95
____*Black Eyed Peas: Unauthorized Biography*, ISBN #: 978-0-9790976-4-5, $16.95
____*Red Hot Chili Peppers: In the Studio*, ISBN #: 978-0-9790976-5-2, $16.95
____*Dr. Dre In the Studio*, ISBN#: 0-9767735-5-4, $16.95
____*Kanye West in the Studio*, ISBN #: 0-9767735-6-2, $16.95
____*Tupac Shakur—(2Pac) In The Studio*, ISBN #: 0-9767735-0-3, $16.95
____*Jay-Z…and the Roc-A-Fella Dynasty*, ISBN#: 0-9749779-1-8, $16.95
____*Your Body's Calling Me: The Life & Times of "Robert" R. Kelly*, ISBN#: 0-9727519-5-52, $16.95
____*Ready to Die: Notorious B.I.G.*, ISBN#: 0-9749779-3-4, $16.95
____*Suge Knight: The Rise, Fall, and Rise of Death Row Records*, ISBN#: 0-9702224-7-5, $21.95
____*50 Cent: No Holds Barred*, ISBN#: 0-9767735-2-X, $16.95
____*Aaliyah—An R&B Princess in Words and Pictures*, ISBN#: 0-9702224-3-2, $10.95
____*You Forgot About Dre: Dr. Dre & Eminem*, ISBN#: 0-9702224-9-1, $10.95
____*Divas of the New Millenium*, ISBN#: 0-9749779-6-9, $16.95
____*Michael Jackson: The King of Pop*, ISBN#: 0-9749779-0-X, $29.95

Name:_____

Company Name:_____

Address:_____

City:_____State: _____Zip:_____

Telephone: (_____)_____E-mail: _____

For Bulk Rates Call: 602-743-7211   **ORDER NOW**

❏ Check ❏ Money Order ❏ Cashiers Check
❏ Credit Card: ❏ MC ❏ Visa ❏ Amex ❏ Discover

CC#_____Expiration Date:_____

Payable to:
    Amber Books
    1334 E. Chandler Blvd., Suite 5-D67
    Phoenix, AZ 85048

Shipping: $5.00 per book. Allow 7 days for delivery.
Sales Tax: Add 7.05% to books shipped to Arizona addresses.

Total enclosed: $_____

www.ingramcontent.com/pod-product-compliance
Lightning Source LLC
Chambersburg PA
CBHW051832090426
42736CB00011B/1766